Praise for *The Leader's Guide* to *Mindfulness*

'What a refreshing book! . . . the mindful....ss approach to creativity is really great. Audrey is not falling into the trap of telling people to be creative without explaining clearly how to do it. She makes it easy to take the first steps and to develop creative potential with clear explanations, efficient tools and fun exercises, relying on multiple solid sources and on her vast experience in the corporate world. Audrey will help open your eyes to see the true capacities you have inside and unleash your creative superpowers through her clever mindfulness approach.'

Butzi, TED speaker, magician and author, *The Magic of Crazytivity*

'By retrieving the essence of mindfulness from the jibber-jabber of pop psychology, Dr Tang has penned a triumph. Concise, practical . . . indispensable.'

Peter Karataos, Consultant Clinical Psychologist and clinical adviser, PeakHealthOnline.com

'A timely book for anyone who wants to bring out the best in themselves – and others – using simple, effective techniques. Tang's highly readable style makes this a book that can be dipped into again and again, with observations and examples that inspire. Read it for a more enjoyable, more mindful life!'

Lucy Beresfordo writer, broadcaster and psychotherapist

'A practical, easy-to-read book which allows the reader to understand and apply the techniques of mindfulness straight away. Through a range of accessible exercises, Dr Tang offers leaders a "mind oasis" to benefit and support performance.'

Dr Monomita Nandy, Senior Lecturer in Accounting, Post Graduate Director, Brunel Business School, Brunel University

'Workplace wellbeing continues to be high on the agenda of all serious businesses and public sector services. In *The Leader's Guide to Mindfulness*, Dr Tang expertly navigates the fact and fiction, separating gimmick from meaningful practice ensuring the reader can drive forward evidence based change'. 'You will find this book both scholastically thorough and eminently practical and I highly recommend it.'

Rich Atterton, Association of School and College Leaders, Council Member

'Packed with practical tools and exercises, this book is an essential read for any leader who values wellbeing both in themselves and in their organisation.'

Sharon Lawton, Director, Natural Flair Coaching Ltd

The Leader's Guide to Mindfulness

Pearson

At Pearson, we believe in learning – all kinds of learning for all kinds of people. Whether it's at home, in the classroom or in the workplace, learning is the key to improving our life chances.

That's why we're working with leading authors to bring you the latest thinking and best practices, so you can get better at the things that are important to you. You can learn on the page or on the move, and with content that's always crafted to help you understand quickly and apply what you've learned.

If you want to upgrade your personal skills or accelerate your career, become a more effective leader or more powerful communicator, discover new opportunities or simply find more inspiration, we can help you make progress in your work and life.

Every day our work helps learning flourish, and wherever learning flourishes, so do people.

To learn more, please visit us at **www.pearson.com/uk**

The Financial Times

With a worldwide network of highly respected journalists, *The Financial Times* provides global business news, insightful opinion and expert analysis of business, finance and politics. With over 500 journalists reporting from 50 countries worldwide, our in-depth coverage of international news is objectively reported and analysed from an independent, global perspective.

To find out more, visit **www.ft.com**

The Leader's Guide to Mindfulness

How to use soft skills to get
hard results

Audrey Tang

 Pearson

Harlow, England • London • New York • Boston • San Francisco • Toronto • Sydney • Dubai • Singapore • Hong Kong
Tokyo • Seoul • Taipei • New Delhi • Cape Town • São Paulo • Mexico City • Madrid • Amsterdam • Munich • Paris • Milan

PEARSON EDUCATION LIMITED
KAO Two
KAO Park
Harlow
CM17 9NA
United Kingdom
Tel: +44 (0)1279 623623
Web: www.pearson.com/uk

First edition published 2019 (print and electronic)

Pearson Education is not responsible for the content of third-party internet sites.

ISBN: 978-1-292-24840-0 (print)
         978-1-292-24841-7 (PDF)
         978-1-292-24842-4 (ePub)

British Library Cataloguing-in-Publication Data
A catalogue record for the print edition is available from the British Library

Library of Congress Cataloging-in-Publication Data
A catalogue record for the print edition is available from the Library of Congress

10 9 8 7 6 5 4 3 2 1
24 23 22 21 20

Front cover images © Malsveta/iStock/Getty Images Plus and Omela/iStock/ Getty Images Plus

Print edition typeset in 9/13 pt Melior Com by Pearson CSC
Print edition printed and bound in Great Britain by Ashford Colour Press Ltd, Gosport, Hampshire.

NOTE THAT ANY PAGE CROSS REFERENCES REFER TO THE PRINT EDITION

Contents

About the author

Audrey is a chartered psychologist (CPsychol), and the author of Pearson's *Be A Great Manager – Now* (Book of the Month July 2016 in WH Smith Travel Stores.). She is a CPD accredited speaker, trainer and qualified FIRO-B and NLP practitioner. She is the founder of CLICK Training, where she practices as a development coach and training consultant, and is the resident psychologist on the *Chrissy B Show* (Sky191), the only UK TV programme dedicated to mental health and well-being.

Her doctorate focused on the training and emotional support of customer-facing professionals. During her research she lectured on Brunel University's Business Undergraduate and Management courses, and subsequently trained as a coach within the NHS. Prior to training and coaching, she was a secondary school drama teacher and Head of Psychology (QTS), later progressing to programme manager for vocational qualifications in Supporting Teaching and Learning, and Childcare, Learning and Development within Further Education. She also runs a community theatre group, CLICK Arts, with the aim of using the arts to build confidence.

Her book *Be a Great Manager – Now* has since been licensed to 'Skill Pill' online learning and translated into Russian, Arabic and Chinese. CLICK Training is also currently the only CPD accredited training provider for Team Building using 'Escape Rooms', and she delivers her 'Team Trials' programme with partners in Germany, Switzerland and Greece.

Publisher's acknowledgements

We are grateful to the following for permission to use copyright material:

Text

010 WNYC Studios: Note to Self Podcast (2018) 'Dan Harris Knows All Your Excuses for Not Meditating' https://www. wnyc.org/story/dan-harris-meditation-skeptics. Accessed 12 January 2018. 012 Hachette Book Group: Kabat-Zinn, J. (2016). Wherever you go, there you are: Mindfulness meditation for everyday life'. 012 Parallax Press: Thich Nhat Hanh (2013). Moments of Mindfulness: Daily Inspiration. New York: Parallax Press. 012 W. W. Norton & Company: Siegel, D. J. (2007). The mindful brain: Reflection and attunement in the cultivation of well-being. New York: W.W. Norton. 004 Taylor & Francis: Bodhi, B. (2013) What does mindfulness really mean? A canonical perspective cited in Williams, M.G. and Kabat-Zinn, J.(2013) Mindfulness: Diverse Perspectives on Its Meaning, Origins and Applications, Routledge. 005 Harvard Business Publishing: Goleman, D. (2017) 'Here's What Mindfulness Is (and Isn't) Good for', Harvard Business Review, https://hbr.org/2017/09/ heres-what-mindfulness-is-and-isnt-good-for. Accessed 9 October 2017. 009 Harvard Business Publishing: Goleman, D. (2017) 'Here's What Mindfulness Is (and Isn't)Good for', Harvard Business Review, https://hbr.org/2017/09/heres-what-mindfulness-is-and-isnt-good-for. Accessed 9 October

2017. 012 Harvard Business Publishing: Su, A.J. (2017) '6 Ways to Weave Self-Care into your Work Day', Harvard Business Review, https://hbr.org/2017/06/6-ways-to-weave-self-care-into-your-workday. Accessed 12 December 2017. 013 Harvard Business Publishing: Su, A.J. (2017) '6 Ways to Weave Self-Care into your Work Day', Harvard Business Review, https://hbr.org/2017/06/6-ways-to-weave-self-care-into-your-workday. Accessed 12 December 2017. 020 Hearst Communications, Inc: Papert, S. (1997) In Interview, SFGATE, http://www.sfgate.com/news/article/SUNDAY-INTERVIEW-Seymour-Papert-Computers-In-2856685.php. Accessed 2 February 2018. 021 Whitbred S & Greene N: Whitbred, S. and Greene, N. (2017) 'Byron's Babbles', blog, https://byronernest.blog/2017/04/04/decision-making-vsproblem-solving-and-why-the-difference-matters/. Accessed 16 January 2018. 021 Whitbred S & Greene N: Whitbred, S. and Greene, N. (2017) 'Byron's Babbles', blog, https://byronernest.blog/2017/04/04/decision-making-vsproblem-solving-and-why-the-difference-matters/. Accessed 16 January 2018. 024 Carmichael: Carmichael, A. (2017) 'The Drunken Man', lecture notes, PMI Conference, July, Athens. 028 Taylor & Francis: Dow, G.T. & Mayer, R.E. (2004). Teaching students to solve insight problems. Evidence for domain specificity in training. Creativity Research Journal, 16,4 389-402 033 Scott Barry Kaufman: Aronson, E. (2017) 'Not By Chance Alone', The Psychology Podcast, November. Accessed 3 January 2018. 033 Foundation for a Mindful Society: Jazaieri, H. (2014) 'Can Mindfulness Improve Decision Making?' https://www.mindful.org/can-mindfulnessimprove-decision-making/. Accessed 16 January 2018. 033 SAGE Publications: Hafenbrack, A.C., Kinias, Z. and Barsade, S.G. (2013)'Debiasing the Mind Through Meditation: Mindfulness and the Sunk-Cost Bias' SAGE Journals, http://journals.sagepub.com/doi/abs/10.1177/0956797613503853. Accessed 16 January 2018. 045 Penguin Random House: Quoted in Peter's

Quotations: Ideas for Our Time. Laurence J. Peter. Bantam Books, New York NY, USA. 1977/1979. Page 25. 046 Insider Inc: Marshall, D. (2013) 'There's a Critical Difference Between Creativity and Innovation', http://www.businessinsider.com/difference-between-creativity-and-innovation-2013-4?IR=T. Accessed 31 January 2018. 046 Foundation for a Mindful Society: Goh, C. (2016) 'How to Apply Mindfulness to the Creative Process', https://www.mindful.org/apply-mindfulnesscreative-process/. Accessed 31 January 2018. 049 Pfannkuch K: Pfannkuch, K. (2015) 'The Psychological Reasons People Don't Share Their Ideas', Kapost Blog, https://marketeer.kapost.com/why-people-dont-share-ideas/. Accessed 31 January 2018. 053 Foundation for a Mindful Society: Schiermeyer, E. cited in Goguen-Hughes, L (2011)'Mindfulness and Innovation', https://www.mindful. org/mindfulness-and-innovation/. Accessed 6 January 2018. 054 Foundation for a Mindful Society: Schiermeyer, E. cited in Goguen-Hughes, L (2011)'Mindfulness and Innovation', https://www.mindful.org/mindfulness-and-innovation/. Accessed 6 January 2018. 068 Rodney King: King, R. (1992) Cell phone recording from the Los Angeles Riots, 1 May, https://www.youtube.com/watch?v=1sONfxPCTU0. Accessed 6 February 2018. 076 Thomson Reuters Corporation: Berkrot, B. (2016) 'Biden announces US project to promote cancer data, Reuters, https://www.reuters.com/article/ushealth-cancer-genome-idUSKCN0YS1UN. Accessed 4 July 2018. 087 Udemy: Excellence Assured (2017) NLP training course, lecture notes from the NLP Practitioner Training Course. Course completed June 2017. 091 International Universities Press: Freud A (1937) The Ego and the Mechanisms of Defence, London: Hogarth Press and Institute of Psycho-Analysis. (Revised edition: 1966 (US), 1968 (UK)) 094 Philosophy Now: Yacobi, B.G. (2012) 'The Limits of Authenticity', Philosophy Now, https://philosophynow.org/issues/92/The_Limits_of_Authenticity. Accessed 4 July 2018. 096 NLP World: NLP World (2018) NLP Training – META

Model https://www.nlpworld.co.uk/nlp-training-meta-model/. Accessed 4 March 2018. 109 Kanter: Kanter, R.M. (2005) 'How Leaders Gain (and Lose) Confidence',Leader to Leader, 35 (21–27). 110 McGraw-Hill Education: Meshanko, P. (2013) The Respect Effect: Using the Science of Neuroleadership to Inspire a More Loyal and Productive Workplace, McGraw-Hill Education. 121 Lamott: Lamott, A. (2018) '77 Self-care quotes to remind you to take care of yourself', https://www.developgoodhabits.com/selfcare-quotes/. Accessed 23 February 2018. 125 Health Media Ventures, Inc: Altshul, S. (2012) 'The Healing Power of Pine', Health.com, http://www.health.com/health/article/0,,20428734,00.html. Accessed 28 March 2018. 142 The British Psychological Society: Wasylyshyn, K.M. and Masterpasqua, F. (2018) 'Developing self-compassion in leadership development coaching: a practice model and case study analysis', International Coaching Psychology Review, Vol. 13 (1) 21–34. 144 Guardian News and Media Limited: Burkeman O (2013) Happiness is Reality over Expectations, The Guardian https://www.theguardian.com/lifeandstyle/2013/oct/12/happiness-reality-expectations-oliver-burkeman (accessed 16/2/18) 145 The Foundation for a Mindful Society: Mindful.org (2016) Mindful.org. Accessed 23 February 2018. 146 Penguin Random House: Wiseman R (2003) the Luck Factor, Arrow Books 149 Moodjuice: NHS Scotland (2018), 'Challenging unhelpful thoughts' http://www.moodjuice.scot.nhs.uk/challengingthoughts.asp. Accessed 17 February 2018. 163 University of Wisconsin Press: Hegel, G.W.F. cited in in Davis, W.A .(1989) Inwardness and Existence Subjectivity in/and Hegel, Heidegger, Marx, and Freud, University of Wisconsin Press. 164 European Association of Work and Organizational Psychology: Furnham, A. (2013) 'The Dark Side of Leadership Management Derailment', EAWOP conference talk: http://www.eawop.org/ckeditor_assets/attachments/416/worklab_2013_adrianfurnham_talk2.pdf?1384979822.

Accessed 3 April 2018.) 168 Harvard Business Publishing:
Sinoway, E.C. (2010) 'No, You Can't Have it All', Harvard
Business Review https://hbr.org/2012/10/no-you-cant-have-
itall. Accessed 3 April 2018. 171 Oath Inc: d'Aubermont
Thompson, N. (2017) 'Mindful of Myself: A Brand New Me?',
Huffington Post, https://www.huffingtonpost.com/natalie-
daubermont-thompson/mindful-of-myself-a-brand-
newme-_b_9044772.html. Accessed 3 April 2018. 181
Tyndale House: Ziglar Z quoted in Ziglar Z, Reighard D
(2013) The One Year Daily Insights with Zig Ziglar, Tyndale
House Publishers Inc 182 Penguin Random House: Maslow
AH (1971) The Farther Reaches of Human Nature , New York
183 The Nation: Wijebandara C (2016) The Buddha's Concept
of Leadership, The Nation, http://www.nationmultimedia.
com/opinion/The-Buddhas-concept-of-leadership-30286428.
html (accessed 11/4/18) 184 John Wiley & Sons: Mindful
Leadership: The 9 Ways to Self-Awareness, Transforming
Yourself, and Inspiring Others by Maria Gonzalez 185 Samuel
French Ltd: Rice R, Andersson B, Ulvaeus B (1986), Chess:
The Musical, Samuel French Ltd 185 Harvard Business
Publishing: Argryis C (1986), Skilled Incompetence, Harvard
Business Review https://hbr.org/1986/09/skilled-
incompetence (accessed 25/7/17) 192 John Quincy Adams:
John Quincy Adams 195 FranklinCovey Co: Work-Life
Balance: A Different Cut, by Stephen R. Covey ,© 2007
FranklinCovey Co. 198 Apartment Therapy, LLC.: Velden D
(2015) How to make a Chocolate and Vanilla Swirled Marble
Cake @Kitchn https://www.thekitchn.com/how-to-make-
marble-cake-cooking-lessons-from-the-kitchn-191768
(accessed 13/4/18) 199 Windhorse Publications: The
Dhammapada, chapter 1, verses 1 and 2. Translation by
Sangharakshita, available for free download at www.
sangharakshita.org (accessed 13/4/18) 201 University of
Cambridge: Allen TD, Paddock EL (2015) How being mindful
impacts individuals' work-family balance, conflict, and
enrichment: A review of existing evidence, mechanisms and

future directions, Mindfulness in Organizations, Cambridge 206 Warren Gamaliel Bennis: Bennis WG (2014) quoted in Kandavalli P (2014), Thoughts on Business, Leadership and Christian Life, Wordpress https://paulkandavalli.wordpress. com/2014/08/03/warren-bennis-quotes-on-leadership-and-management (accessed 9/4/18) 211 Wah Seong Press: Seet CK (1961) Discourses on Buddhism, Wah Seong Press, Malacca 211 Wah Seong Press: Seet CK (1961) Discourses on Buddhism, Wah Seong Press, Malacca

Photos

016 Pearson Asset Library: SunnySideUp/Shutterstock 022 Pearson Asset Library: KlektaDarya/Shutterstock 022 Pearson Asset Library: KOUNADEAS IOANNHS/Shutterstock 028 Pearson Asset Library: Dmitry Elagin/Shutterstock 103 Pearson Asset Library: Dmitrij Skorobogatov/Shutterstock 105 Pearson Asset Library: litabit/Shutterstock 116 Pearson Asset Library: szefei/123RF 122 Pearson Asset Library: FotoYakov/Shutterstock 125 Pearson Asset Library: Quang Ho/Shutterstock 052 Shutterstock: Normana Karia/ Shutterstock Back Cover Nick Freeman: Nick Freeman.

Introduction

The opening questions:

▌ What do you think when you hear the term 'mindfulness'?

▌ What do you believe 'mindfulness' involves?

▌ How might 'mindful practice' contribute to your performance as a leader?

The problem with mindfulness

Mindfulness has become so mainstream it seems to have lost meaning.

'Note to Self' Podcast, 2018

Whenever I ask the question of what mindfulness means, around 50 per cent of my audience will invariably say, 'meditation', 'breathing' and 'awareness' – sometimes, they also add 'yoga'. The other 50 per cent will call it 'hokey' and not wish to hear any more.

Yet, the concept has been embraced within the contemporary business environment, even universities are adding a 'Mindfulness in business' course to their programmes, and there is a consistent flow of articles citing big names like Google, Apple and Intel celebrating the organisational gains that 'mindfulness' brings – whether individuals like it or not.

The benefits often are espoused in blogs, news articles and research papers and, to date, including mindfulness in day-to-day working results in:

▌ stress levels dropping

▌ sleep quality improving

▌ pain dropping

▌ an estimated '. . . $3,000 per-employee increase in productivity for the company each year'

(Gelles, 2015)

▌ improved creativity, well-being and focus

▌ stronger enthusiasm in projects and meetings

(Intel Press, 2013)

▌ improved decision making

▌ becoming better listeners

(Gelles, 2012)

▌ better focus and open mindedness

▌ better collaboration

▌ a climate of '. . . openness, acceptance and empowerment'

▌ emotionally and intellectually available leaders

▌ a switch from 'hurried multitasking and its psychological blind spots, to one of curiosity, flexibility and opportunity.'

(Williams, 2016)

The evidence is clear that organisations are onto something by incorporating 'mindfulness', so why do so many still need convincing?

According to Barnett, '"lunchtime wellbeing sessions" now appearing in some companies and institutions are – if they are doing anything at all – just making people docile' (Barnett, 2015). Worse still, rather than incorporate mindfulness as an additional benefit, some US organisations have been providing their employees with mindfulness training *in place of* holiday entitlement or financial benefits (Whippman, 2016).

Further, the big names within the field of mindfulness cannot agree on what mindfulness actually is and how it is practised:

> *Mindfulness means paying attention in a particular way: on purpose, in the present moment, and nonjudgmentally.*
>
> Jon Kabat-Zinn

> *Mindfulness shows us what is happening in our bodies, our emotions, our minds, and in the world. Through mindfulness, we avoid harming ourselves and others.*
>
> Thich Nhat Hanh

> *Mindfulness in its most general sense is about waking up from a life on automatic, and being sensitive to novelty in our everyday experiences. With mindful awareness the flow of energy and information that is our mind enters our conscious attention and we can both appreciate its contents and come to regulate its flow in a new way.*
>
> Daniel J. Siegel

However, their continued prominence comes with substantiating research findings that there are huge benefits to mindfulness within organisations (even if the concept is still somewhat unframed, uncodified, and gives rise to scepticism of '. . . the hippie stuff' (Confino, 2014).

Therefore, it seems that the 'problem' of mindfulness is not that it does not work – but that it is *misunderstood*. As such, while this book will cover the background theory of mindfulness and explain its usefulness to the leader, it will approach the field in a much more contemporary way – by *applying* the techniques.

How this book works

Each chapter opens with self-reflection prompt questions and includes practical mindfulness exercises and meditations focused on the topic at hand. (Many of these activities can be done alone, with your team, or as part of an organisation-wide workshop.) To progress your learning further, chapters conclude with a toolkit, offering a reminder of the key points, challenging you to introduce simple mindfulness into your day, and developing some of the techniques used within the chapter. Of course, some theory is essential – you may want to convince a board to implement mindfulness sessions or workshops, or perhaps make changes to the working day to enhance well-being, therefore the exercises are con-textualised through an overview of the background research; but, as to tangible benefits – they will be best achieved through practice. Let the academics continue to argue principles, mindfulness works in its application – and you, the leader who can incorporate its techniques, will reap the rewards.

The meditations referred to in this book are included in transcript form for your own use in workshops, and are availble exclusively to you as recordings at the following link: www.draudreyt.com/meditations (Password: leaderretreat).

Voice: Dr Audrey Tang
Accompaniment: Mr Simon Gargrave, simongargravemusic. co.uk

part 1

Practical applications

The mindful leader

The opening questions

▌ What is the perception of mindfulness in your organisation?

▌ What approaches to mindfulness have you experienced?

▌ If you have experienced mindfulness techniques – were any of them helpful to you?

A s a leader who wishes to include mindful practice professionally, it is helpful to have a sense of what it is and where it comes from; if nothing else, but to convince the sceptics of your credibility on the topic!

Where does mindfulness originate?

It was in 1979 when the Stress Reduction Clinic at the University of Massachusetts presented the 'Mindfulness Based Stress Reduction' programme (MBSR), which brought the Buddhist practice of meditation into the formal scientific and clinical setting.

MBSR, in its use of the term 'mindfulness', acknowledged its practice within Buddhism. The practice of mindfulness is the seventh factor of the eightfold path, one of Buddhism's

'Four Noble Truths'. Through *mindful* meditation for transcendence, Buddhists attained:

▍ '. . . a state of peace and bliss'

▍ '. . . contemplation of one's own experience, subsumed under the four objective domains of the body, feelings, states of mind, and experiential phenomena'

▍ '. . . greater compassion'.

(Bodhi, 2013)

As such, the meditation practised within MBSR was also focused on those three elements:

▍ a peaceful emotional state

▍ awareness and balance of the body and mind

▍ compassion (for the self and other).

The course, still popular today, comprises a mix of meditation retreats where participants focus on yoga-breathing and broadening awareness of their bodies.

When it first appeared on the scene, this unification of 'East meets West' as a form of treatment generated interest, but, as the term 'mindfulness' grew in popularity, so did the need to formally evaluate the science behind it. Buddhism would be accepting of practice enabling self-reported transcendence; science needed more to be convinced.

The growing literature on mindfulness included development of the MBSR work of Jon Kabat-Zinn (widely credited for the popularity of mindfulness) and the use of formal meditation and focused breathing began to yield results:

▍ Reports of a better work–life balance (e.g. Shanafelt *et al.*, 2012; Michel *et al.*, 2014).

▍ Improvements in resilience (e.g. Keye and Pidgeon, 2013; Pidgeon and Keye, 2014).

▌ Performance benefits for leaders, such as improvements in compassion and collaboration (e.g. Ling and Chin, 2012; Trisgolio, 2017).

As the interest grew, more books were written on the topic to encourage the practice to spread, and organisations started taking an interest as a means of improving the performance of their staff.

Unfortunately, what is also clear is that many books on mindfulness, in trying to convince leaders to implement it, would often focus on explaining the neuroscience behind the concept, for example: the improvement of neural pathways and circuitry in the brain (e.g. Davidson and Lutz, 2008). This was all too easy to criticise due to lack of verifiable evidence. 'In particular', said emotional intelligence writer Goleman in 2017, there is a lack of fit to the 'gold standards for medical research'. Such damning words in sceptical industry papers and scientific journals meant the leader who embraced it might choose to invest in it (and sometimes their passion would inspire their teams to give it a go) but many would not.

Arguably, mindfulness aside, it has long been known that simple deep breathing can make a huge difference to performance. At the very least, this element can be demonstrated.

Try the following exercise.

EXERCISE 1.1

What are your levels of stress or calm?

Take note of your current level of stress or calm:

Very stressed   5   4   3   2   1   Not stressed
at all

Sit comfortably with your hands in a relaxed position in your lap

Take a deep breath in through the nose for a count of three

Hold it for three

Release it slowly by breathing out through the mouth for a count of six

Repeat the process five times

Take note again of your level of stress or calm:

Very stressed   5   4   3   2   1   Not stressed
                                                   at all

Hopefully, you will perceive a greater level of calm following the exercise.

Physiologically, our levels of anxiety are regulated by the parasympathetic nervous system (PNS) and the sympathetic nervous system (SNS). As we breathe in, blood is drawn to the lungs and the heart responds to this deficit (using the SNS) by pumping more around the body. As we exhale, the PNS slows the heart down because the deficit is reduced. The body is efficient at maintaining the balance in a healthy heart. However, under stress, breathing becomes shallow and erratic, which means that both systems are trying to work but find it harder to reach equilibrium. However, the act of slow, relaxed, deep breathing has the added effect of activating the 'slow adapting pulmonary stretch receptors' (SARs), which inhibit the working of the SNS so it does not increase the pumping of the heart muscle (MacKinnon, 2016). Therefore, slow, deep breathing is effective in inducing calm.

However, mindfulness can bring more than that. It is not just about calming the mind through breathing exercises or meditation, it can include techniques for clearing and re-energising the mind too.

How a clear mind improves organisational performance

One of the disadvantages of the frantic multi-tasking world in which we live – and which leaders are often trained to improve their skills within – is not being 'fully present' within everything that needs to be done. How many times have you been talking to a friend, a spouse, your child and found yourself distracted by your phone, tablet or laptop? The balance that leaders need to strike is between quality and quantity – in life and in work.

In his book *High Performance Habits,* Brendan Burchard (2017) spoke of an executive who seemed able to handle a complex and extremely tight schedule and still offer engaged and high performance. Burchard identified that, in between each item on the list, the executive would perform a mental palette cleanse. In between running from one meeting to another, he would go to the bathroom, splash his face with cold water and do a couple of star jumps. He would complete one task before moving to the other. Burchard tried it for himself and found he could engage more with each new task. In the same way as a wine connoisseur might sip water or eat a dry cracker between tastings so as not to affect the taste of the new wine with any flavour of the old – if a leader is able to afford him or herself a 'mind cleanse' between tasks, engagement will be refreshed for the next.

Try this exercise.

EXERCISE 1.2

Imagine you have to send a series of emails, then go to a meeting, then go to another meeting.

1. After you have completed your emails, splash some water on your face, take a couple of deep breaths or do some star jumps to clear your mind prior to your next engagement.

> 2. After the meeting, do the same.
>
> You will find that you will be re-energised for the start of that next task.

At the very least, doing this means that you are still completing all your tasks – but are giving each a higher quality of attention.

Although this technique would not necessarily be classified under 'mindfulness', it is, arguably, a good means of improving your 'embodied awareness'. Thus I posit now that any technique aimed at improving awareness, compassion or balance that may be of benefit to performance may fall within the realm of 'mindful practice' . . . and, without any clear codification of the term 'mindfulness' as yet, if it works – use it!

So what does mindful practice entail for the leader?

A report by The Mindfulness Initiative (2016) presents *a series of mindfulness interventions* and reviews undertaken by Cranfield, Birmingham and Aberystwyth Universities, resulting in organisational self-reports of participants:

- feeling more focused
- experiencing an improvement in behavioural insights
- moving forward rather than brooding

A team that is able to do this will be of benefit to any organisation.

Following this, Daniel Goleman recanted his earlier concern and conceded that, following a literature review of the studies, there are many discrepancies in the academic rigour;

however, there is still enough evidence to suggest that, 'while you shouldn't believe everything you hear about mindfulness, there are, indeed, payoffs . . . ' (Goleman, 2017).

Taking the application of the common mindful techniques (breathing, meditation and exercises for awareness) a step further, research by Tang and Carr (2018) suggests that *any* intervention that improves self-awareness can be beneficial to executives. They ran a 10-week 'Mindfulness Programme' for leadership and management students at Brunel University following a session structure of:

▮ positive affirmations

▮ breathing exercises entitled 'Yoga breathing'

▮ theory about the technique being used

▮ practice

▮ reflection and feedback

▮ guided meditation

and found that participants reported improvements in the categories codified through Bodhi (2015):

▮ embodied awareness

▮ emotional balance

▮ compassion

as well as in

▮ confidence

▮ ability to relax

▮ creativity

▮ clarity in decision making

Exercises and techniques within the programme included activities inspired by neurolinguistic programming (NLP) and psychology as a means to elicit a greater awareness of the self – some of which are also included in this book.

As such, it is arguable that the scope of 'mindful practice' extends beyond meditation and breathing and – even better – can be adaptable to how the leader wishes to incorporate it into the organisation.

How can I apply mindfulness as a leader?

Rather than approaching mindfulness as a buzzword, it is most effective when incorporated into daily life. It is not essential to introduce 'meditation lunch hours' but encouraging your teams to do some deep breathing (or any 'mind' cleanse activity) before they enter a meeting can cleanse the mind and raise their performance and credibility (Mudd, 2015). This concept can be seen in practice within the McLaren Honda Technology Centre where all staff have to pass through a completely white corridor before entering the workplace (MAHLE Powertrain Ltd, 2017). The relative openness of the concept means it is possible for the leader to be creative in applying mindful practice, and this book will offer suggestions as to how this may be done.

Therefore, one of the most effective ways in which a leader can apply mindfulness is through its use in common parlance – 'Just be mindful' – be *more aware*.

Whether this is helped by mindful meditation, deep breathing, yoga or any of the exercises and techniques in this book – including merely being told to 'be more aware' – if an exercise is effective, or if you tweak it and it is effective, *then utilise it.*

With multi-tasking a necessary part of leadership, and invaluable to keeping up with the fast-paced world, leadership development focuses on being able to attend to numerous demands and display a range of skills simultaneously (Williams, 2016). Mindfulness seeks to improve not the number of skills a leader has but the *depth and quality* of those skills in performance.

Think of your abilities/traits on a scale. Outline them in no particular order.

FIGURE 1.1 An example using the commonly cited leadership skills/traits

Those who are experienced or natural leaders may have a longer scale than those who are just starting or learning. But, whether you are already practised or just starting out, you have the capacity to develop more.

The difference between taking a *mindful* approach to leadership and any other leadership training is not in making the scale longer, but by adding depth.

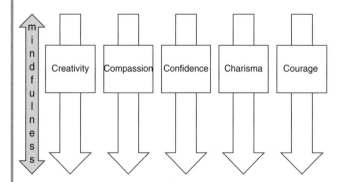

FIGURE 1.2 Adding depth to the commonly cited leadership skills/traits

By incorporating mindful practice to enhance your self-awareness, you will refine the leadership skills you already have, as well as develop further your emotional agility to adapt as needed – either using what you have or through fostering innovation.

Mindfulness also functions as a form of self-care

It is getting more and more common to introduce well-being and self-care into books aimed at the high-flying executive. The reason is simple: the higher you fly, the harder you work, but the faster you may become exhausted. One means of developing your longevity at the top is through self-care.

Self-care may be defined as '. . . care provided "for you, by you". It's about identifying your own needs and taking steps to meet them. It is taking the time to do some of the activities that nurture you. Self-care is about taking proper care of yourself and treating yourself as kindly as you treat others.' (Fort Garry Women's Resource Centre, California, 2018). It is also one of the most important elements of longevity in leadership. No matter what your skill, if your health forces you to retire, you can no longer demonstrate it. According to Su (2017), self-care is no longer '. . . a luxury; it's part of the job'.

Every day as a leader comes with pressure. Significant decisions have to be made – which have far-reaching consequences; the threat of competition is always lurking; alliances may need to be formed, which may or may not serve you long term; further, as an emotional agile leader, often you will have a team who – with open lines of communication – will seek your advice as they need to; and, of course, you will also have a fulfilling life outside the workplace, which needs maintenance and attention. This is emotionally draining.

Su (2017) lists the four detrimental behaviours into which leaders slip when self-care is not part of their routine:

▎ self-neglect

▎ self-management

▎ self-sabotage

▎ self-preservation

Because of the frenetic pace at which a leader's life may move – not forgetting that those who are successful in the workplace often have success in their personal lives (an area that needs to be looked after too) – it is essential for the leader to remain authentic, grounded and recharged. It is in these very areas that mindfulness plays a part. Permeating all walks of life with no restriction on age nor belief system, this practice offers everyone – particularly the leader – some respite, often achieving a better balance and resilience at home and in the workplace (Mindfulnet.org, 2017).

Mindful practice has the potential to enhance *emotional agility* – the ability to be aware of your emotions as well as adapt them to the needs of others; and *resilience* – the ability to pick yourself up again following setbacks *and* continue to perform at your best for everyone else, whether you are making decisions, problem solving, creating or innovating, providing support or building relationships. It has a place professionally and can enhance your personal well-being too.

Let the academics concern themselves with framing and codifying mindfulness. The techniques in this book will support and enhance your performance and that of your team.

IN SUMMARY

1. Despite there being some question marks over the exact science and framing of 'mindfulness', research shows it has very successful applications.

2. In addition to (rather than a substitute for) leadership skills, it can help sift through the white noise to get an accurate view of the various options in a given situation.

3. Mindful practice brings depth and breadth to your current leadership skills, thus improving performance.

4. It helps teams remain open to new ideas – from wherever they may generate – and also to draw easily from their own resourcefulness.

5. Mindfulness encourages a mindset of openness and compassion, conducive to successful collaboration, and it promotes a culture of help and assistance rather than envy and competition. It teaches you to reframe failure so that you may learn and grow; it encourages gratitude to appreciate where you are in the present – and how much you can become in the future.

6. Emotional agility within the pressures of leadership needs support and self-care to avoid exhaustion.

7. To garner the benefits, mindful practice is about raising awareness of the self and others – which, in turn, creates a clear platform for creativity, decision making and learning, and this can be applied in any way that best suits your organisation.

8. These benefits do not only benefit the working professional, but also extend further into your own personal life.

9. And remember, whatever your final approach to incorporating mindful practice, mindfulness must always be *additional* to good basic organisational procedures already in place, otherwise this can give rise to 'pseudo growth' – something that can be detrimental and unhealthy (Maslow,1970).

CHAPTER 1 TOOLKIT

▮ Mindfulness remains a contemporary issue in leadership.

▮ Companies who have introduced mindfulness into their working practice have reaped rewards in performance, but it is still viewed with scepticism.

▮ This chapter introduced the leader to the history of mindfulness and its application within the business world.

Key points to remember

1. *Always* remember mindfulness can help clear much needed space within your busy schedule and practise a 'mind cleanse' or take time to breathe deeply before rushing to the next thing.

2. *Sometimes* take a moment to recognise how your body is feeling.

3. *Try* to introduce a short time for mindful practice into your day (even if it is 10 minutes before bed).

Take action

1. **Reap the benefits of deep breathing**

See what a difference it makes when you take a couple of deep breaths just before starting a presentation. As you do, remind yourself of the first line you will use to open your talk. This will give you a moment to find clarity and begin speaking with power and impact.

2. **Improve your energy when multi-tasking**

Make a conscious effort to cleanse your mind in between tasks:

▍ Before you go into your second/third/fourth meeting of the day, take a moment to 'shake out' so you can walk in re-energised.

▍ In between emails, try to stretch your arms up (hold for eight) and stretch your legs out in front (hold for eight).

▍ Go to the toilet when you need to and, while there, splash some water on your face before you return to your next task.

Small acts of re-energising will make you better able to concentrate at the start of your next task and enhance your productivity.

What I tried

Date	Action

What worked for me

Date	Action

Please use a separate piece of paper if necessary.

Meditation techniques
Mindful relaxation

As you begin this guided meditation, remember this is time for yourself. Switch off your phone and move away from your computer. Make sure you are somewhere you will not be disturbed. This is your time to relax and recharge so that when you return to sharing your time with others, you will feel happier, healthier and more energised.

As you begin to relax, focus first of all on your breathing. Start to take deep breaths in through your nose, hold for a moment, then breathe out through your mouth. With each breath you are breathing in cool, energising air and breathing out stresses and tension. With each breath you feel more and more relaxed.

Focus on your breathing – breathing in cool, energising air and breathing out tension. As you breathe out, let that sense of relaxation flow through your feet – releasing all the tension. Now let the feelings of relaxation flow through your knees to your ankles and through your feet. Now let it flow through your legs, relaxing your body as it goes. Through your torso – recharging you, relaxing you. Then downwards from your neck, through your torso, your legs and out through your feet, relaxing you as you breathe and, finally, relax your head, your shoulders and arms, your body your legs and your feet – calm, cool, relaxed, allowing the air you breathe in to re-energise you while keeping your mind at peace.

Just breathe – enjoy that sensation.

Now think about somewhere special to you – it might be a special place on a holiday, it might be in your home, it might be somewhere in your imagination or from your past – wherever it is, take a moment to picture it now. Still relaxed, still re-energising.

Picture that place – feel how warm and comfortable you are there. Think of the people – or even animals – or perhaps objects that are special to you in that place. This is a safe place, a warm place – and it is your place.

Enjoy your special place where you are relaxed and able to recharge.

Remember you can come back to this special place whenever you feel like it – you can shut your eyes, concentrate on your breathing and think about it, or you can replay this guided meditation.

But it is your place. A special place. A safe place. A place that allows you to feel warm, comfortable and just like you again.

As you picture that special place, feel the warmth, the comfort – the energy coming from that place. And let it wash over you. The energy from that special place relaxes and recharges you ready to face whatever is ahead of you. This special place is yours, it is somewhere that you can go to recharge because you can draw from that energy.

Let the energy flow through you from the room, you are still relaxed and you are recharging. As you breathe in, you feel more and more refreshed, more and more energised, more and more recharged. This is because you took some time just for you.

Enjoy that feeling for a moment longer. Breathe in the energy and, as you breathe out, relax and enjoy the sensation of feeling just like you again.

Breathe in – hold – breathe out.

Breathe in – hold – breathe out.

You are relaxed and energised.

Now you will start to return from that special place and begin to get ready to step forward into your day, fully recharged and refreshed.

Remember you can come back at any time.

I will begin to count backwards from 10 and, as I do, I will ask you to become more and more aware of your surroundings, still feeling relaxed and recharged.

10, 9 – start becoming aware of your feet and the ground, maybe wiggle your toes and move your ankles.

8, 7 – become more aware of where you are sitting or lying, how that feels against your body.

6, 5 – become aware of your arms and hands – wiggle your fingers – stretch out your arms – feeling nice and refreshed and relaxed.

4, 3 – become more aware of the sounds around you. Start to move your neck and your head.

2, 1 – when you are ready, you can open your eyes ready to go about your day.

Problem solving and decision making

The opening questions

▮ Do you know the difference between problem solving and decision making?

▮ What biases do you have that might impact on your decision making or approach to problem solving, i.e.:

  ▮ in framing the problem

  ▮ in deciding on and actioning a solution?

Applying mindfulness to problem solving and decision making

Now more people are doing work that requires individual decision-making and problem-solving . . . we need an educational system that will help develop those skills.
Seymour Papert, 1997

Leaders need to make decisions every day. You may already have a method, a strategy or, perhaps, you rely mostly on past experience? Mindfulness helps you to recognise the limits of your knowledge as well as become more aware of your biases, values and objectives (Reb *et al.,* 2014). It looks at the importance of separating relevant information from 'white noise' in order to come to a decision in which you can be confident; and challenges you to focus on the 'real' delay (i.e., the one that is going to cost us the most in real (measurable) hardship – loss of revenue, loss of client). Instead, you may have a preference to focus on the one that has 'got your goat' or 'the one you find easiest to address' when it comes to problem solving.

While both decision making and problem solving are related, it is important for the leader to distinguish between the two, as some mindfulness techniques are helpful for enhancing awareness overall, but others are more specifically related to either making a decision or solving a problem. Also, using the wrong process can hinder both – and affect your credibility at the same time.

The differences between problem solving and decision making

While 'both problem solving and decision making involve using information to inform an action' (Whitbred and Greene, 2017), problem solving involves finding the root cause of an issue and resolving it, but, while the outcome is clear – the problem must be resolved – the process of resolution cannot be started until the root is found.

Decision making has no need to seek the root – it is a choice between different causes of action. Contrary to problem solving, the process is clear, each option must be evaluated based on relevant parameters, but the outcome becomes clear only once the decision has been made.

To illustrate this further, for Whitbred and Greene (2017), 'A detective is a problem solver . . . their objective is clear. Their journey is not clear.

A judge is a decision-maker. Their journey is clear . . . but their purpose is not . . . '

Problem solving is finding a cause, decision making is choosing between options already laid out – however, once the cause is found, decision making often is needed in taking the action to address the problem.

. . . and why the difference matters

In taking a mindfully aware approach to business practice, a leader who uses (or applies) the terms interchangeably can hinder both the process and the outcome. Not only that, but it can have detrimental consequences for the executive who gets it wrong.

Try the following.

EXERCISE 2.1

You are the only person with the authority to promote someone. You have conducted the interviews and you have collected the feedback.

What do you do?

Sometimes leaders – especially inexperienced ones – fear making a decision and want to consult with other managers. However, treating a decision as a problem can result in 'decision by committee', which includes input from people who do not necessarily understand your team's needs, and can be a waste of everyone's time. This can also result in others losing confidence in you because of your reluctance to take action – it can even be perceived as a reluctance to take responsibility.

Now try the following.

EXERCISE 2.2

You need to cut costs within the department, and it has been suggested by colleagues senior to you that redundancies are in order.

What do you do?

In this case, it may be more mindful to have a look at the budget and discuss with your team areas where you can make cutbacks. In one NHS team where this occurrence happened, the leader realised she could save the required amount of money through training her team to deal with waste appropriately. Treating a problem as a decision might result in creating further problems, for example in this case, redundancies may have resulted in a shortfall in staff leading to burnout of the team who remained.

How do I know which approach to take?

Sometimes, it is clear whether an issue is a decision or a problem – but a simple rule of thumb is:

▌ If I know what outcome I want (but do not know the options to get there) – it is a *problem*.

▌ If I have to evaluate between options (but cannot control the outcome) – it is a *decision*.

Mindful problem solving

Once you have decided that you need to take a problem-solving approach (decision making is part two of this chapter), your next task is to frame the problem so your team can solve it. Many find this difficult to do well and, when you take a look at the psychological biases that can impede the process, it is easy to understand why.

How to frame a problem for your team

Start with the *reality,* not what you presume the problem is.

Too often, because of past experience, you may choose to tackle what you assume a problem to be. This makes sense – you will have dealt with similar situations in the past and your team may explain the issue clearly. However, sometimes, it can be mindful to observe the situation for yourself – even if it is just through a Skype video call.

Relying solely on the reports of others may not be deliberately misleading, but their perception may be askew. For example, it is very easy to be misled by unconscious beliefs that may arise through past experience – something common for the reflective executive.

Try this exercise.

EXERCISE 2.3

You will need a six-sided dice or the dice app on your smartphone/computer.

Instructions

A drunken man is walking from point A to point B.

A ————————————————————————— B

Your rolling of the dice will trace his path.

You will roll 24 times.

If you roll an even number (2, 4, 6), the man walks upwards. If you roll an odd number (1, 3, 5), the man walks down.

For each role, make a mark on the line, for example:

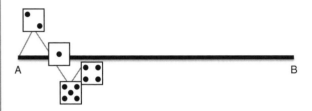

Before you start – *predict*

How many times do you think he will cross the centre line in 24 rolls? _____

A _____ B

Actual number of times he crossed the line: _____

(Carmichael, 2017)

Were you accurate?

Did you predict he would cross the line 12 times?

The law of averages – which most of us will have used to predict (albeit unconsciously) – would have us presume he will cross the centre line about 12 times, but, in reality, as he gets further and further away from the line, it becomes harder to return.

This same analogy may be applied to framing a problem.

If you start at the point at which you *believe* the problem to be, your unconscious biases – i.e. the 'rules' which you use unconsciously to make predictions – may mean you do not look for the root. For example, you may assume that a problem raised between two team members is due to a personality clash and, if past experience has shown you that it will 'blow over', you may respond accordingly. But, in this case, it might need investigating, so the action taken through experience may be only a short-term, or an inappropriate, solution.

As stated earlier, it does not mean that past experience will not serve you well. Just be mindful that there may be something else happening, which may need you to take a moment to investigate.

By being aware that unconscious preconceptions – including experience – may affect your judgement, you will be better able to recognise, and address, any cognitive misconceptions or biases.

Three commonly held misconceptions and biases that affect problem solving
Are you guilty of this sort of thinking?

▍ My system is 'fool proof' because I can be aware of it 100 per cent of the time.

▍ I know my team is doing what they should be doing – because I am doing what I should be doing.

▍ The bigger fish is always the threat.

As leaders, you have to have the courage of your convictions and, therefore, having confidence in your ability, your team and your perception of competition is necessary, to some extent. However, if confidence crosses into arrogance, or your ego becomes dependant on it, it can affect your ability to problem solve (General Colin Powell, 2011).

It is important, therefore, to learn from experience, but remain open minded when using it to guide your future behaviour. It may be that there are eventualities which you did not predict that negatively affect the new outcomes of your 'rules of thumb'.

'My system is fool-proof'

EXERCISE 2.4

Thought experiment

Mobile phones are not to be used when driving because they can create a distraction. Adverts currently show what happens when one is distracted by replying to a text. However, you may think, 'That's texting. If I don't text, what's the problem? . . . having a conversation is not the same.'

But, what happens if you drop your phone?

If you firmly believe that you can be 100 per cent diligent and therefore your performance is beyond reproach, your supposition is erroneous. Humans are fallible . . . and, the bigger the system they are managing, the worse this can be (Carmichael, 2017).

'My team is doing everything they should be, because I am . . . '

Similarly, if you believe your team is doing everything they 'should' be, just because you are, you have again fallen prey to egocentrism. Everyone is egocentric to some degree, but it is important to remain aware that seeing the world only through your perception is a cognitive bias, which can result in – like the drunken man example – missing the root of a problem.

Try this exercise.

EXERCISE 2.5

Use a piece of string or a tie or a ribbon – or a laced shoe, if you have one.

Describe how to tie a shoelace into a bow to someone – however, that person is only to follow your instructions.

How did it go?

Not only do others not think like you, but they may not even use the same terms as you to describe the same object or action. Always observe for yourself what is actually going on.

And what if you think your problem is '*the bigger fish*'?

This is a commonly held belief because of constant reports of, for example, large corporations or retail parks damaging the local shops on the high street. Media and film have long since espoused the bigger firm exploiting the little person. However, Carmichael (2017) suggests that it is the 'faster fish' that may prove to be the real threat. If you have a good idea, chances are someone else will have it too, and it is as much a race to see who gets it out there first before who shouts about it the loudest. Be aware, especially when a problem generates a fear, that you know accurately what the threat is.

Mindfully framing the problem is an excellent start, and mindfulness also has an effect on coming to a solution.

Mindfulness and 'insight problems'

This chapter has not yet mentioned 'meditation'. This is because meditation can help, but only with very specific types of problems.

Ostafin *et al.* (2012) identified two types of problems:

▌ insight problems, i.e. those which need a 'eureka' moment

▌ non-insight problems, i.e. those which past experience can assist with or that can be 'worked out'.

An 'insight' problem

For example, the nine dots problem.

Join the nine dots with four straight lines without taking your pen off the paper

FIGURE 2.1 The nine dots problem

A 'non –insight' problem

For example, the tower of Hanoi.

FIGURE 2.2 The Tower of Hanoi

Your task is to move all the blocks from the far left spoke to the far right, finishing with them in the same order as pictured, in as few moves as possible.

Leaders can, indeed, use experience to address the second sort of problem but, with regard to the first, are often at the same level as a novice, as the solution is one that is 'inspired' rather than worked through.

Ostafin *et al.* (2012) found that a 10-minute meditation resulted in faster problem solving of the insight problems compared with a control group who heard a 10-minute natural history lecture. In a development of this research, he explained further that because the process of problem solving was habitually 'verbal-conceptual', i.e. what we tell ourselves about the problem directs our approach to the problem, this can hinder the generation of insight. In other words – how the problem is framed (which can rely on your language or even language limitations) can affect how solutions are sought.

While this book will examine the effect of mindfulness on creativity and innovation in the next chapter, it is worth mentioning here that a brief mindful meditation can help clear your mind in order to allow insights to form.

Try this exercise.

EXERCISE 2.6

If you are struggling with a problem, try the following:

1. Go to www.draudreyt.com/meditations and play the 'mindfulness for problem solving' track.

2. Or/And state the problem, including:

   ▪ what it is

   ▪ when and where it occurs

> ▮ who it involves
>
> ▮ how it happens (is there a pattern?)
>
> ▮ what outcome you want to see.
>
> (Chang, 2012)
>
> **3.** Outline your possible solutions.

When a problem needs you to evaluate the solutions, or strategies in reaching those solutions, then you need to move to the process of decision making. Again, mindful practice can assist.

Mindful decision making

If you need to make a decision, or the solutions generated to your problem have brought you to the point of choosing a path, mindfulness can assist decision making in the following ways:

▮ framing the decision

▮ gathering information

▮ coming to a conclusion

▮ learning from feedback.

First, however, a little bit of reflection can even help you decide '. . . if a decision is necessary' (Insead Knowledge, 2014). Then, mindful techniques can make you aware of your biases in forming your judgement.

Framing the decision

Be aware of your emotional bias in decision making.

In *The Happiness Hypothesis,* Haidt (2006) likened rational thought and emotion within decision making to a rider and an elephant. He asked, 'Which is leading?' He represented rational thought as the elephant and posited that its strength and size enables it to overcome emotion. However, the rider (the representation of emotion) will still lean a certain way and thus influence the path.

However, some questions are not ones of choosing rationality over emotion, but ones of understanding which is the most important to the outcome. If choosing a house, then rational thought may be the more important, the same is harder to be said when it comes to choosing a romantic partner.

If your feelings are central to the decision, it is likely that rational thought and evidence may still do little to persuade you. Mindfulness can help you get to identify what is driving your choice and, even if you still wish to be led by emotion, it is a conscious move.

Further, truthful awareness of what your desires are means it is possible to gather information and form a conclusion more successfully because you are looking for *appropriate* evidence – not just seeking evidence to validate what you want.

Try this exercise.

EXERCISE 2.7

While it is certainly not advisable to allow important decisions to rest on the flip of a coin, if you are making a decision, be clear in your mind which would be heads and which would be tails and flip the coin. *Without* looking at the coin, once it is flipped, do a 'mini scan' and see if you can become aware of which outcome your body had the preference for.

Without looking at the coin, start gathering information with that in mind.

Gathering information

Look for the 'null hypothesis' – seek evidence against your bias and try to overcome it.

Elliott Aronson (2017) spoke of his concern with the 'TEDification of Psychology' – the idea that scientists were using only the validating parts of their own research to promote a 'pop psychology book'. Aronson advised, when gathering information to make a decision, it is always best to 'look for the null hypothesis'. This same practice can be applied to the information-gathering element of mindful decision making.

Rather than looking for evidence which supports the decision you are erring towards, look for what may refute that path. Once you have formed the arguments against that direction, try to refute those.

If you are able to overcome that and still wish to go that way, then this is most likely to be the best decision for you.

Avoid the 'sunk-cost' bias (Hafenbrack *et al.*, 2013)

A 'sunk-cost' is something that has already '. . . happened in the past, not the present nor the future' (Jazaieri, 2014). Jazaieri (2014) gives the example of a long-term relationship which is not happy, but the couple prefer to stick together because of the number of years already passed. He explains that it is natural to want to see a return on our investments – especially time – and to hope that holding on that little bit longer might yield positive results. Unfortunately, those who have been through this know that this is rarely the case. Within the organisation, this may be a business relationship that is not working or feeling unhappy with a job you have done for a long time and not progressed in. Hafenbrack *et al.* (2013) found that a series of 15-minute meditations focusing on deep breathing '. . . reduced the tendency to think in sunk-costs . . . [and] . . . reported . . . less influence by past events in making decisions.' Hafenbrack et al. (2013) suggested that mindful meditation '. . . decreased focus on the future and past, which reduced negative moods and emotions, which in turn led to reduced sunk-cost bias.'

When faced with letting something you have invested in – but seen little result from – go, it can be difficult to cut that tie. For example, you may have championed someone during your recruitment process but, even after all the support they have been offered, they are still under performing. While you may be reluctant to let them go, it is also important to be aware of the impact that keeping them may be having on the rest of your team or the organisation.

To help you move from the feelings of 'sunk-cost' try this exercise.

EXERCISE 2.8

Go to www.draudreyt.com/meditations and play the 'Five senses meditation' track or the 'Body scan' track.

These tracks are quick to listen to before you go to sleep or when you wake up. The more you practise these, the more aware you will become of the present – which, in turn, will decrease your focus on the past. In making decisions, while there is no guarantee that a choice will result in a positive outcome, it will, nonetheless, give you an opportunity; repeating the same behaviour over and over again definitely will not bring anything new.

Coming to a conclusion

Consider this: you have limited time and resources to complete three tasks for a client, how do you decide where to start?

Some leaders may have a system in place, some leaders may leave it to their experienced team, but how can you tell if the comfort zone bias will not affect your decision, i.e. a focus on the task you like or find the easiest, rather than the one that is the most necessary?

Try this exercise.

EXERCISE 2.9

Outline the three tasks.

From knowing your team – rate the effort it will take out of 10.

From speaking with the client – rate the importance for the client out of 10.

Now do the same with the other tasks, and use the resulting values to assist with your decision making (Soonevelt, 2017).

This is how it might look.

Task 1	Task 2	Task 3
Effort = 9	Effort = 3	Effort = 3
Importance = 8	Importance = 8	Importance = 3

By making often internalised views visible and (albeit arbitrarily) measurable, it is sometimes easier to make decisions on allocation of resources. It is also a reminder that it is important to include the narrative from the client in your judgement. In the above example, it is arguable that you need to start with task 1 because it takes more effort, then task 2, which is easier to complete, yet still as important, leaving task 3 till last. When done in collaboration with those involved, this is more effective – it may be that your team says it would be best to start with task 2 to 'get it done'.

However, what this protects against is doing task 3 first – especially if it is the most enjoyable, or because someone who is quite influential in the team 'really wants to do it'.

While you may be thinking, 'But I've got no time for that' – in the same way as any practice can become habitual – mindful practice can become habitual too. It probably took a bit of time before driving your car became 'automatic'. Habits take practice to form; how much more effective would your practice be if those habits were all positive ones?

Learning from feedback

Evaluate your decision in context.

Should you choose to override that decision at a later date, be mindful that you took the original decision for good reason *at the time*. Life is dynamic, times can change and with them priorities. It is not necessarily that your decision-making process was faulty, but that you are now at a different juncture with different priorities.

IN SUMMARY

1. Problem solving and decision making are two different processes. However, mindful awareness can assist with both, and in not confusing the two.

2. Personal and emotional biases, as well as past experience, can affect our ability to problem solve or make judgements clearly. Mindful meditation or deep breathing can help clear the mind.

3. The narrative of a situation from different perspectives can assist in making decisions, as can making a thought process visual and objective.

4. Always learn from reflection and feedback after you have solved a problem or made a decision. However, you must also evaluate that reflection with attention to the context in which it was made.

CHAPTER 2 TOOLKIT

▮ Leadership skills training does not always differentiate between decision making and problem solving, yet, getting it wrong has detrimental repercussions.

▮ The mindful leader observes this distinction and is able to make executive decisions with confidence and problem solve with clarity, avoiding emotional and cognitive biases.

Key points to remember

1. *Always* remember that problem solving and decision making can be compounded by biases.

2. *Sometimes* reflect, when problem solving or decision making, on which way you are 'leaning' to try and identify your biases.

3. *Try to* tackle problems and decisions from the *realistic* starting point – although further investigation takes time, it may yield more effective results.

Take action

1. **The freer your mind, the easier the solution**

Next time you are faced with a problem or decision, take a moment to look around and observe. Consciously use all

your senses to engage with your surrounding – sight,
sound, smell, taste, touch.

Approach the problem with this same openness.

2. Look for the 'null'

When making a decision, instead of listing just the pros
and cons, try listing all the cons first and arguing against
them.

It is always easier to find something to support your
choice, but, if you take the time to examine your
arguments (through looking at those which do not support
you), you can be surer in your eventual decision.

What I tried

Date	Action

What worked for me

Date	Action

Please use a separate piece of paper if necessary.

Meditation techniques
Guided deep breathing

This is a simple guided breathing exercise. This may help
you if you just want to centre yourself during the day or
perhaps you want to use it as part of your routine to go to
sleep at night.

Find a comfortable place where you will not be disturbed. Sit
or lie down and close your eyes. We will do five rounds of
breathing; you will breathe in through your nose for a count
of three, hold for two, then out through your mouth for five.
It is a simple, relaxing task and will help calm your mind and
centre your emotions.

Breathe in through your nose – two, three.
Hold two.
Out two, three, four, five.

And again:

Breathe in through your nose – two, three.
Hold two.
Out two, three, four, five.

As you breathe, feel the tension slipping away.

Breathe in through your nose – two, three.
Hold two.
Out two, three, four, five.

You are breathing in cool, calm, cleansing air
Breathe in through your nose – two, three.
Hold two.
Out two, three, four, five.

You are breathing out tension.
Last time:

Breathe in through your nose – two, three.
Hold two.
Out two, three, four, five.

When you are ready, you may open your eyes.

Five-senses relaxation

This is a simple guided relaxation that raises your awareness of all the information coming in through your senses, making you more aware, more alert and observant in your performance. Sit or lie in a comfortable position. Switch off your phone, close your computer and make sure that you will not be disturbed.

To begin, you will take three deep breaths – breathing in through your nose for three, holding for two then out for five.

Again, in through your nose, hold for two and out for five, four, three, two, one.

Once more, in through your nose, hold for two and out for five, four, three, two, one.

Carry on breathing in your own time, while I take you through this five senses relaxation.

Focus first of all on what you can visualise in your mind. See the room in your mind, try to be as detailed as you can. What is in front of you, what is to the side of you, what will you see if you look up, look down, look under? Don't worry if it's all unclear now, you can check and clarify it later on. Whatever you are picturing in your mind, make that image really clear – really bring it in focus. Think about the colours of what you can see, the angles, the lines – make them really bright and vibrant. Make what you see really sharp and clear.

Breathe in through your nose, hold for two.
Out through your mouth four, three, two, one.

Breathe in through your nose, hold for two.
Out through your mouth four, three, two, one.

Now focus on what you can hear. What sounds are around you? Is there chatter? Traffic? Can you hear the whirr of the lights, a projector or something different? Can you recognise any of those sounds? Are they loud, soft? Focus on the differences between the sounds – are they happy, playful, hard working? Focus for a moment on the sounds in the distance then turn your attention to the sounds nearby – breathing, rustling of fabric, the creak of the chair. Lots of sounds making up our daily life.

Breathe in through your nose, hold for two.
Out through your mouth four, three, two, one.
Breathe in through your nose, hold for two.
Out through your mouth four, three, two, one.

Focus on what you can taste – perhaps you need a drink? Perhaps you are hungry or maybe you have had a lovely meal?

Breathe in through your nose, hold for two.
Out through your mouth four, three, two, one.

Now think about what you can smell. Fresh air from outside? Perhaps food is being prepared? Maybe you can smell something completely different? What are all those smells around you? What do they tell you about your environment? The people?

Breathe in through your nose, hold for two.
Out through your mouth four, three, two, one.

And now think about what you can feel – the fabric on your skin, your body resting against your seat or whatever you are lying on. Are you warm, cool, what sensations surround you right now?

We don't often take the time to think about what we can take in from all our senses – and yet we can learn so much and find a lot of pleasure from them. Next time you are walking out on a sunny day, take a moment to listen to the birdsong, or feel the warmth of the sun on your skin, maybe even smell the flowers. When you eat or drink, take a moment to really enjoy the taste.

Breathe in through your nose, hold for two.
Out through your mouth four, three, two, one.
Breathe in through your nose, hold for two.
Out through your mouth four, three, two, one.

And slowly become more aware of the room as you get ready to go about your day.

When you are ready, open your eyes.

Body scan

It is best to do the body scan lying down. It is a great relaxation to do, especially before you go to bed. If you want to, you may record what you notice during the body scan in a journal with the date of your scan.

Find a comfortable place where you will not be disturbed. Make sure you have switched off any communication devices. Lie down where you are comfortable.

We will begin the body scan with three deep breaths – let each breath relax your body more and more.

Breathe in through your nose for three, hold for two, then out for five.

Again, in through your nose, hold for two, and out for five, four, three, two, one.

Once more, in through your nose, hold for two, and out for five, four, three, two, one.

Carry on breathing in your own time, while I take you through the body scan.

Focus first on your toes. Wiggle them then relax them. Notice the difference between when you are moving them and when they are at rest. Focus on them for a moment. How do they feel?

Breathe in through your nose for three, hold for two, then out for five.

Now move your awareness to your ankles. Wiggle them and relax them. How do they feel? What do you notice, if anything, about your ankles?

Breathe in through your nose for three, hold for two then out for five.

Move your awareness to your knees and shins – what are you feeling?

Breathe in through your nose for three, hold for two then out for five.

Now scan your thighs – how do they feel? Do you notice anything?

Breathe in through your nose for three, hold for two then out for five.

Scan your pelvis and hips. Relax them. Notice how they are feeling.

Breathe in through your nose for three, hold for two then out for five.

Move your awareness to your stomach. How does that feel? What about when you relax it?

Breathe in through your nose for three, hold for two then out for five.

Now your chest. How is your chest feeling as you breathe in and out? Gentle and relaxed?

Breathe in through your nose for three, hold for two then out for five.

Scan your shoulders and the tops of your arms – as you think about each body part, acknowledge it and relax it. Release any tension in your shoulders – if you carry tension there, where exactly do you carry it?

Breathe in through your nose for three, hold for two then out for five.

Scan your arms from your elbows to your wrists and down to your fingers. You might want to wiggle then relax them – how are they feeling?

Breathe in through your nose for three, hold for two then out for five.

Now scan your neck and chin – sometimes we grit our teeth or hold tension in our jaws without even realising it – how do they feel? Relax them. How do they feel now?

Notice the difference between tension and relaxation.

Breathe in through your nose for three, hold for two then out for five.

Finally scan your face and your head – relaxing them as you do so. What do you notice?

Breathe in through your nose for three, hold for two then out for five.

You can conduct this body scan in place of a meditation or to relax you before bed. It will help to make you more aware of what is going on in your body and help you recognise when something is wrong or different and you can make a note of it to follow it up afterwards.

Breathe in through your nose for three, hold for two then out for five.

Breathe in through your nose for three, hold for two then out for five.

When you are ready, you may stretch and open your eyes. Be careful when you stand or continue focusing on your breathing to send you off to sleep.

3

Creativity and innovation

The opening questions

▐ Are you more or less creative now compared with when you were a child?

▐ Are you more or less curious now compared with when you were a child?

▐ Are you a creator or an innovator? (Do you prefer to *think* or *do* . . . and could you do both?)

Be mindful of the difference between *creativity* and *innovation*

> *Every child is an artist. The problem is how to remain an artist once he grows up.*
>
> Pablo Picasso

The creative freedom and innate curiosity enjoyed by the child is consistently reduced as they pass through the education system. This is not only through rules or development targets shaping the actions of the child, but a reduction in opportunities for creative pursuits with subjects such as drama, music and art being squeezed out of the curriculum (Jeffreys, 2018, BBC News). When the leader seeks to engage creativity and innovation from his or her team, they can be faced with not only blank stares, but fear. Taking a mindful approach can help alleviate this and reignite the flame of inspiration.

In the previous chapter, the differences between *insight* and *non-insight* problems were discussed, so too must the difference between *creativity* and *innovation*. This is because: 'Organisations often chase creativity, but what they really need to pursue is innovation' (Marshall, 2013) . . . and, conversely, sometimes, creativity is hindered by the desire for innovation.

Creativity is:

▌ subjective

▌ immeasurable.

Innovation is:

▌ introducing change into a relatively stable system

▌ the work needed to make an idea viable (the *application* of the creative resource).

(Marshall, 2013)

The two terms often are used interchangeably, as an innovation starts with a creative idea. However, this chapter will look at the effect of mindfulness on:

1. The generation of creativity.

2. The process of applying the idea to invoke change.

Mindfulness and the creative process

Goh (2016) defines creativity as '. . . producing something new and useful'. She breaks the processes of the creative brain into four processes:

▌ preparation

▌ incubation

▌ illumination

▌ verification.

She further suggests that mindfulness plays a large role, especially in the first three stages (while making us more accepting of criticism in the fourth). Schootstra *et al.* (2017) suggest that 10 minutes of mindful meditation prior to brainstorming can enhance results and Goh (2016) emphasises how heightened awareness can help within the incubation and illumination period as you are developing the idea.

However, it is notable that, while you may subscribe to this idea in theory, finding the time and space for meditation before brainstorming can be difficult, especially if teams are remote and time is short. But, research suggests that the act of mindful meditation (even without direct focus) can still reveal improvements in creativity, even if teams learn the technique and practise it before bed (Shallard, 2017).

Ask yourself:

▌ Do you believe you are open to everything around you?

▌ Do you believe yourself to be wholly observant?

The first part of exploring creativity is to remember that, even for the person who feels they 'aren't creative', inspiration can come from everything around you – if you choose to observe it.

Try this exercise.

EXERCISE 3.1

You need to offer a report on what is around you – including your periphery. Look around you for 30 seconds.

What did you see?

_____

_____

_____

_____

Did you notice everything that was going on?

Really?

> How confident are you that you have a full picture of your immediate environment?
>
> But did you look up?
>
> What about down?
>
> What did you hear? Smell? Feel?

Even when instructed to observe your peripherals, you will not always consider looking up or down. Even less likely are you to think about smells, sounds or touch (Beardsley, 2016). Yet, so much information can be gleaned from a full observation which makes use of all the senses. Fixing the draught by closing the door is less effective when there is a hole in the roof. Practising mindfulness just reminds us that there may always be more to consider.

One simple instruction: 'Remember to look up/down' or 'Remember to think about all your senses' can make a big difference in sparking a creative idea.

Now try this.

EXERCISE 3.2

[1]You have to fill each box with a different picture in three minutes.

Try it:

---

[1]This is an adaptation of an exercise in Wiseman, R. (2004) *Did You Spot the Gorilla? How to Recognise the Hidden Opportunities in Your Life.* Arrow.

How did you get on?

How about if you think of the following:

▌ What might inspire a picture if you think about the sky or the ceiling?

▌ What might inspire a picture if you think about the floor?

▌ How might a smell inspire a picture? A taste? A touch?

When directed, it is easier to find a spark of inspiration which can then lead to even more ideas. In his example of this exercise, Wiseman directed his teams to think about what a child might draw or what an astronaut might draw to inspire ideas.

If you sometimes reject creative tasks because of low self-belief in your talent, this task enables you to draw inspiration from a different perspective. This can also be helpful when you are looking at a problem from the point of view of the client; and it will be something which the section on 'Jugaard' will also acknowledge.

Dealing with emotional biases in creativity

Sometimes, generating the creative spark is not enough; the leader also has to overcome emotional biases when it comes to expressing the team's creative thinking.

1 Preparation

'People think "What if my idea is a total flop?" or "What if someone steals it and makes millions?"' (Pfannkuch, 2015). These are two of the main reasons why people do not like to express ideas. A third is 'But it's not realistic.' This can sometimes hold you or your team back from verbalising any ideas.

First, it is important to recognise that people can have similar ideas all the time. But, to move from an idea to implementation (and innovation), someone has to do the work to execute it successfully. This also tackles the issue of '. . . but it's not real' because you are separating the wish to 'make it' from the request to '. . . come up with an idea'. In asking his team to design a 'phone with one button', Steve Jobs did not look for realism at first, he looked for concepts.

The first hurdle of developing creativity and innovation is getting your team to generate, *then* communicate their ideas *in order* for them to be implemented. Mindful practice can help generate the 'safe space' for teams to express themselves without fear of ridicule.

Try this.

EXERCISE 3.3

During a brainstorming session, participants are asked to stand in a circle. Tell them that you are holding an invisible ball. The ball will 'become' an object of your choice and you will throw it to someone in the circle. They must acknowledge the object that you have chosen before they change it, name it and throw it to someone else.

For example:

I am holding the ball and I say, 'It's a cat,' – I throw it to person B.

Person B 'catches' it and says, 'It's a cat,' and then says, 'It's a spear,' and throws it to person C.

Person C catches it and says, 'It's a spear,' and then says, 'It's an alien,' and throws it to person D.

What you sometimes find is that not only is this a fun game, but that participants start acting out catching the object.

While this allows a sense of childhood freedom, which is always conducive to the creative process, you can then debrief the group by explaining that not only were you encouraging creativity, but the most important part was the *acknowledgment of the idea of the other person first before you changed it to your own idea.* This encourages teams to listen to each other, as well as acknowledge that ideas often are inspired by something else.

If you have time to meditate prior to a brainstorming session, there is a short 'Meditation for creativity track', which can be downloaded. Go to https://www.draudreyt.com/meditations. Mindful meditation can reawaken the almost child-like freedom of creativity (Goh, 2016) – too often stifled as adults – which broadens the mind to other possibilities.

2 Incubation

As an idea develops, it will undergo changes. At this point, Goh advises that simple meditation can also help prevent 'obsessing' during the incubation stage, and encourage openness to criticism in verification, which can assist in development of an idea rather than defence of the same.

Sometimes, it can help if teams are able to appreciate the effect of defensiveness on stifling creativity. While the next chapter will focus on collaboration and teamwork (and any exercises are applicable here), this is a simple exercise to facilitate a discussion on the importance of remaining open to idea development.

Try this.

EXERCISE 3.4

In a team session, partners are asked to label themselves A and B. A is to start a conversation using a suggestion. B is to reply, building on that suggestion using 'Yes and . . . '

For example:

A: Let's go to the zoo.

B: Yes and then we can buy some popcorn.

The exercise continues with A building on the suggestions with 'Yes and . . . ' and so on.

Make it clear that the suggestions can be whatever participants like.

Then run the exercise again, this time with A making suggestions, but B always answering with 'No'. This forces A to continue the conversation alone (and then swap).

Explain that this demonstrates how difficult working together can be when there is constant resistance to ideas and suggestions. If you have time, this is a good opportunity to explore why such 'stonewalling' may occur, if it does.

The act of bringing awareness to the way ego can result in 'stalemate' (and sometimes ill feeling, as can be demonstrated) can help teams understand the importance of being open. A further exploration of why someone may be protective of their idea can help create a safe and trusting space where teams are unafraid to share their thoughts and creativity is not stifled by ego.

3 Illumination

Illumination is akin to innovation – the act of putting something into action. Here, teams have the seed, but they need to bring it to fruition. Mindful meditation has brought positive results in dealing with 'insight' problems, so it can be used again at this point to free the mind in order to accept new ideas into the development of a concept.

4 Verification

Again, a common fear in testing an idea is failure, although most sensible executives are not so insecure as to perceive failure as an endpoint. What is important is that you remind them to identify the root of the problem. Root cause analysis, however, often is feared because it happens following failure rather than being something that is embedded within company behaviour. Weick and Sutcliffe (2007) proposed that companies instead create a '. . . mindful infrastructure that continually does all of the following:

1. Tracks small failures

2. Resists over simplification

3. Remains sensitive to operations

4. Maintains capabilities for resilience

5. Takes advantage of shifting locations of expertise.'

(Weick and Sutcliffe, 2007)

This approach meant that making minor mistakes was acceptable, teams engaged in mindful reflection as a matter of course and, most importantly, a proactive approach to actioning ideas was demonstrated so that the task of verification was improved rather than the ability to respond when it went wrong – as it went wrong less (Latino, 2013).

Creativity and innovation can be hugely hindered by your emotions – indeed, seeing something you have cared about fail is heart-breaking. Therefore, it is important to encourage a culture of reflection and revision so that improvements are made as a matter of course. In turn, this is likely to result in a much better finished product or performance outcome.

Mindfulness and innovation

> *Technologies are tools, and you can use them to do great things or not.*
>
> Eric Schiermeyer, 2011

As an echo to the statement that innovation is the act of *doing something* with the idea, Schiermeyer (2011) went on to say: '. . . most successful and innovative tech companies are those that use their own version of mindfulness to listen carefully to what people want and supply it to them.' Schiermeyer does not define what that 'version' might be, but as the section on 'verification' (above) suggests, the most effective innovators have a development process that is '. . . insightful . . . and carefully constructed' stemming from '. . . the cultivation of wisdom practices'. The organisation that works mindfully from the start improves not just the result, but the methods of application of processes or design and, in turn, is the fastest to capture its audience.

Creativity alone is not enough; you have to listen to the needs of your clients, remain sensitive to changes within them and work within a process that takes this all into account – and is flexible enough to adapt as needed. Rather than continually 'pushing' your ideas onto them, find out what they want and incorporate that into your design.

Ask yourself:

▌ Do you know what your clients' needs are?

▌ How have they changed over the last three years?

▌ How equipped are you (professionally and technologically) to address those changes successfully now and in the next three years?

Schultz (2014) suggests that one way to give yourself an innovation mindfulness check is to take a look at the cues within your environment.

Try this exercise.

EXERCISE 3.5

Look around you and make a mental note, not only of what you see, but what it might indicate. If, for example, your workspace is untidy – what might that mean? If you have certain files out – is there a reason for it? If there is something still on a to-do list, what is it a reminder of?

Ask your teams to do the same within their workspaces. What do they notice? Are they lacking certain resources? What effect does this have?

What is the evidence telling you about your organisation at the moment?

Tournier and Ferring (2017) suggested that innovation was also enhanced by avoiding automatic responses and categories. Teams were instructed to note their immediate response, but also to consider an alternative. The same was true when they were asked to offer a solution. This act of mindfulness encouraged a more informative dialogue with clients as well as an awareness of a variety of solutions.

Try this exercise.

EXERCISE 3.6

1. Note your immediate response to a client request, but also consider an alternative response.
2. Note your immediate solution, but also consider an alternative with no restriction (i.e. if money/time/technology were no object.)

Ask your teams to do the same.[2]

_____
[2] This is an adaptation of the task that Tournier and Ferring (2017) proposed.

This will bring you similar information to that which Tournier and Ferring found, but may also offer you ways in which your service could be improved.

If your organisation is equipped, then you are ready to innovate.

Disruptive innovation

There is no point innovating without it making an impact and organisations tend to want to create disruption, placing their innovation at the forefront of their field. There are many ways to do this, but the most straightforward approach is Perry Timms' (2018) 'three-part' method for disruptive innovation:

Innovation at the	Innovation in the	Innovation that is
core	*adjacent*	*transformative*

Innovation at the *core* involves a development of something which already exists, perhaps something central to the business itself. This may involve making a lead product bigger or creating it with a higher specification – or even a new colour – to meet the client or customer needs.

Innovation in the *adjacent* is being aware of the trends within the industry, especially those underground or slightly less mainstream with a following, then bringing the creators into the organisation forming collaboration.

Disruptive, or *transformative,* innovation often involves a leap from the familiar into either new territory or a completely different product. This may derive from adjacent or core innovation, but the move from your current business to the new is less linear.

However, teams – or sometimes other leaders whom you need to convince – are often fearful of transformative innovation as it marks a departure from the familiar, but can sometimes be assisted through the process.

Try this exercise.

EXERCISE 3.7

Play your team (or those you need to bring on side) a piece of traditional music (e.g. Pachelbel's Canon in D major) and ask them what sort of dance would fit with it.[3]

Play a hip hop beat song and ask them what sort of dance would fit with it.

Ask them if a modern style would fit the traditional music and vice versa – would a traditional style fit the hip hop dance?

Ask them what they would do if a client wanted the hip hop style to the traditional music.

---

[3]This exercise is a variation on one presented by Anastasia Tomara at the Learning and Development Conference in Athens, 30 January 2018.

Having done this in my own work, I have found that, despite thinking at first that this 'won't work', teams demonstrate the three-stage process by looking first at the 'core', adapting what they already know, e.g. adding a beat or speeding up the music. Next, they draw from experiences of fusions, e.g. cultures where tradition is commonly mixed with modern. Finally, they are comfortable with proposing something 'disruptive', e.g. proposing 'reversible outfits' or scenery reflecting the styles and they appreciate that often this improves the original piece.

EXERCISE 3.7 CONTINUED

Then play any of the 46 modern songs which feature the Canon which can be found here: www.youtube.com/playlist?li st=PL1F978713F38AD934, particularly *We Dance On* (N-Dubz featuring Bodyrox), if using the hip hop example.

Ask them to think about how the progression of the music occurred and how the dance progressed. Did it happen simultaneously?

What allows the music to fuse?

How have the differing styles (in dance and music) helped create something even more effective?

An excellent song for examining a fusion of a number of hits from the Pachelbel Canon to modern day is *Ladies and Gentlemen We are Floating in Space* by Spiritualized. This may even lead to a discussion on other fusions, e.g. cuisine, fashion, architecture; and go some way to bridging the gap between what your team is comfortable with and progressing into the unknown.

Once your team is better able to accept the fear of disruption because of the progress it makes, greater creativity is entertained and innovation is championed.

Jugaad and innovation

However, the mindful leader is also able to push both creativity and innovation a step further. In their book *Jugaad Innovation*, Radjou *et al.* (2012) discussed the need for an incubator for premature babies in developing countries. The cost for a Western incubator was over $20,000 and, because they needed electricity, this could also prove dangerous. Considerations such as placing babies under lightbulbs were discussed and dismissed on the grounds of safety, so the design team went to see what the needs of the clients were. They realised that the clients in this case were not the doctors in the hospitals, but the families in the villages without any access to electricity. Setting these parameters, they came up with the 'portable infant warmer'. Based on the 'kangaroo care' of keeping the infant in a pouch, this was a sleeping bag with an electric heater.

At only $200, this was an affordable solution.

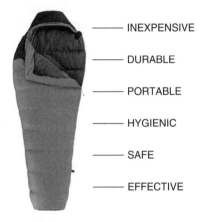

INEXPENSIVE

DURABLE

PORTABLE

HYGIENIC

SAFE

EFFECTIVE

FIGURE 3.1 Portable infant warmer

While not all organisations will face the issue of money, taking a Jugaad approach (subtitled 'frugal and flexible') can be invaluable to the creative – and latter innovative – process. How often do organisations create and innovate in one specific way, just because that's the way it's always done, or just because that's the only way they know?

By setting different parameters, for example, resources, materials, cost and clarifying the specific end user and their needs, you can encourage teams to be flexible with their approach and may create – and innovate – something even more useful than if they had remained on their habitual path.

Further, this practice will encourage your teams to think broadly as a matter of course and, in the same way as the creative spark can be ignited by perceiving through different eyes, what better to innovate frugally than looking at how nature (in this case the kangaroo) might do it.

You will notice that of all the suggestions in this chapter, there is limited use of meditation. However, meditation does have its place in innovation since, as with problem solving, a clear mind is a more capable mind (Barak, 2016). As such, you may wish to use any of the meditations for peace and clarity which accompany this book to generate insight and peace.

IN SUMMARY

1. Mindfulness gives permission to engage in a child-like state of creativity.

2. There is a difference between creativity and innovation. In order to create disruption, you need to have the idea and be able to implement it.

3. Creativity can be enhanced by directed awareness and/or looking through different perspectives. These 'perspectives' are not just those of the client or customer, they can also be of 'a child' or 'an astronaut' or anything – just to stimulate wider thought.

4. Meditation can calm the mind prior to a creative or brainstorming session, but it also enhances insight so, when being able to innovate proses a problem, meditation may help clear the mind for the 'a-ha' moment.

5. Part of a successful creative process is breaking down the psychological barriers that teams have, e.g. fear of getting it wrong or fear of someone 'stealing' their idea. A place for mindful meditation or relaxation helps create a safe space for exploring creativity, as can exercises which teach listening and acknowledgment.

6. Organisations must also keep their implementation processes working efficiently, and mindful awareness can help ensure that problems are reported rather than avoided or ignored.

7. Part of a successful innovative process is to understand the problem that you are trying to solve and generate ideas from there – sometimes using the process of Jugaad for flexibility and clarity of the specific end user.

CHAPTER 3 TOOLKIT

▮ Organisations which understand the difference between creativity and innovation can exploit both; when one is lacking, successes may be fewer or narrow.

▮ However, great leaps in both creativity and innovation can be found in the organisation that utilises ' Jugaad' – frugality and flexibility.

Key points to remember

1. *Always* set yourself up to innovate (but provide the motivation to create through creating a safe space in which to do so).

2. *Sometimes* look around within your field to see what groups may be of help in a creatively 'disruptive' collaboration.

3. *Try to* avoid setting limits or constraints on creativity.

Take action

1. Practise Jugaad

When you are looking to innovate, think about the *purpose* of the creation. Then see if you can identify anything similar in nature.

Nature is often the most efficient worker, so look at what you can learn from its already streamlined processes.

2. **Try 'pull' creativity and innovation** Speak to the client, team or 'end user' about what they need and begin your creative process from that standpoint rather than looking at what other similar organisations are 'giving' to clients or what you think they need.

You might be able to merge your findings, but when you give people what they want – and they can identify as that having been done – they are more positively predisposed.

What I tried

Date	Action

What worked for me

Date	Action

Please use a separate piece of paper if necessary.

Meditation techniques

Meditation for creativity

Find a comfortable place and shut your eyes. Sit relaxed and take deep breaths in and out. As you relax, begin to focus on the sounds around you. What can you hear that you normally filter out? Acknowledge the sound and let it pass. Continue to breathe deeply.

Now think about the sensations that you feel – the feel of the clothing you are wearing – how it sits on your body, the feel of your hands in your lap or on your knees – is your touch heavy or light?

How does the atmosphere feel? Are you pleasantly warm? Cool? Feel the air surrounding you. Now smell that air, what fragrances can you smell – perhaps it's lunch time, perhaps it's the fresh air of the open window.

Now think about what you can taste and how your mouth feels, all the time breathing slowly and gently.

Remember to use as many senses as you can when you are opening your mind to create, there is no right or wrong, only ideas.

Remind yourself that you can you use your awareness of everything around you to help you become more creative.

Slowly, I will count backwards from five and, as I do, you will become more and more aware of everything around you and how it feels, how it looks, sounds, tastes – your senses will be awakened and help you: create, five, becoming more aware of the sounds, four, the smells, three, the tastes, two, the touch, one – you are energised and ready to create.

Meditation for peace and clarity

Make sure you are somewhere you will not be disturbed. Switch off your phone and close your computer. This is a time where you can find peace and clarity without the distractions of the day.

Sit or lie somewhere comfortable.

When you are ready, we will begin this guided meditation.

Start by focusing on your breathing. Breathe in through your nose and out through your mouth.

As you breathe in, you feel the cool, fresh, relaxing air enter your body and, as you breathe out, you breathe out all the stress, tensions and demands of the day.

Breathe in, breathe out. With every breath you relax a little more.

You begin this guided meditation in a beautiful forest. The sun is glistening through the trees, you can hear the birds singing. There is a little stream running by full of fresh sparkling water.

You can smell the beautiful flowers and feel a cool breeze.

You see a small path and begin to walk down it. Feel the grass beneath your feet. Even if the terrain is uneven, you walk with confidence, firmly moving forward.

While you are walking, you can still take a moment to enjoy the beauty around you – the freshness of the breeze, the melody of the birds, the warmth of the sun. You are confident and relaxed.

As you walk, you see a pathway leading up a mountain. You begin to walk upwards – just as confidently as you did in the forest.

The air is fresh, the sun is warm and you walk with strength.

With each breath you are more and more energised.

As you climb higher, the sky gets bluer and your mind gets clearer. Your breathing keeps you energised. Your steps are confident.

You come upon a clearing. It has a beautiful view and a very comfortable place for you to sit.

You are energised by the blue of the sky, the warmth of the sun on the clearing and the colours of the flowers around you.

You sit, comfortable and relaxed.

You breathe that fresh mountain air.

Your mind is at peace here.

You can see things clearly here.

You are safe here.

Breathe that fresh mountain air.

The sun feels warm, the breeze feels fresh and you feel at peace.

Breathe in and out and enjoy that feeling.

You can spend as much time as you like here. This is your place to think. You can come back here whenever you want to.

Breathe in and out and enjoy that feeling of peace.

When you are here, you see things clearly. You observe them as if from outside and this gives you a new perspective.

You can accept what you cannot change yet, and you are energised to take action where you can.

Breathe in the energy of the fresh air, letting it flow through you and breathe out. With each breath you renew your strength and you renew your focus.

Enjoy that feeling for a moment.

When you are ready, you leave the clearing and make your way down the mountain. You keep that feeling of energy with you and you walk with strength and confidence.

Whatever you are facing today – you are strong enough.

As you reach the bottom, notice the firmness of the ground supporting you. Begin to become aware of the room you are in and the firmness of the ground or chair supporting you.

Retain that feeling of clarity and energy as I count backwards from five. Five, start wiggling your fingers and toes, four, start moving your legs and arms, three, awaken your neck and head, two, take a strong energised stretch, one, when you are ready, open your eyes, ready to return to your day.

Relationships and collaboration

The opening questions

▮ What issues have you recognised within inter-team or inter-department collaboration?

▮ What relationships within teams or within departments are positive?

▮ What collaboration or relationship issues at work affect *you* personally?

Promoting mindful relationships

Can we all get along? Can we all get along?

Rodney King, 1992

While Rodney King was speaking on a socio-global issue, the macro world is reflected in the micro. Teams that are unable to 'get along' often find it difficult to pull together to achieve. While teams do not need to be 'best friends', a respect and acknowledgment of each other's value is essential for good performance. Mindfulness promotes acceptance of the self and other, while respecting that each view is valuable – and while we can ourselves learn to collaborate with it, we do not have the right to change it within one another (Excellence Assured, 2017).

Just ask for it!

The MBSR course from Mindfulness Works (2017) suggests that one of the most important things in enhancing collaboration is first to make it clear that collaboration is the aim. When bringing a team together:

▌ identify collaboration as the intention of the group

▌ make it clear that each contribution is valuable, especially as it might be from a perspective different from our own.

However, in remote teams this may not be easy to do consistently.

The problem with collaboration

In 2002 Patrick Lencioni immortalised the five dysfunctions within a team ranging from the absence of trust to inattention of results. When a team was not functioning efficiently, performance would suffer as much as the distorted emotions within the situation.

At the very basis of a team not wanting to collaborate was the absence of trust.

As with not wanting to share their ideas, discussed in the last chapter, it is not uncommon for teams to mistrust each other. This may be due to past experience, to a fear that their personal standards will not be met or even that their work may be undermined or sabotaged. If they already lack confidence in themselves or their ability to be recognised by their leaders, so grows their desire to go it alone – or act with limited input from others. This way they maintain control of their own output and can reap the rewards.

However, as also explored in the last chapter, collaboration brings many benefits – the ability to identify and rectify mistakes sooner, respect for the roles that others play and the skills that they have, and a greater outcome than if one were working alone.

Nonetheless, being forced to collaborate can still result in issues higher up the pyramid, namely a fear of conflict and a lack of commitment. Both can result in lip service being paid to teamwork rather than actual efforts capable of making a difference.

Fear of conflict may be in regard to wishing to maintain a comfortable existence. Even the idea of conflict can cause the stress response to arise in some (if this happens, please engage in the deep breathing exercises in Chapter 1), as such it is sometimes easier to offer the show of being part of the team while choosing not to commit. While this may not have a hugely detrimental effect, a team which is unable to utilise positive conflict to highlight and solve problems, or commit to a joint outcome which has the potential benefit of a team of good brains rather than one or two, also misses out on the benefits.

Lack of accountability and inattention to results are, therefore, what is left for a team which collaboration eludes – a result which will not reach potential and cannot (or will not) be learned from.

So, what is the mindful manager to do?

Encourage greater understanding of the importance of the team through the following:

The scrum

Developed by Takeuchi and Nonaka (1986), the 'scrum' derived from the behaviour of rugby players going in for the ball and getting it back into play. It has been taken under the wing of project management techniques and suggests the implementation of a system where teams give consistent feedback on their work. A daily 'scrum' would:

▐ reflect on what was done since the last scrum

▐ identify the obstacles or any backlogs

▐ set the objectives for the day.

This is not in replacement of a meeting, but it is a fast and effective way to touch base with each area of a project (no matter how remote, as Skype or video conferencing could be used), as well as allowing each team to take responsibility for their role and bringing that information to the scrum.

A scrum, covering those three points, with adequate preparation from each area, should take no longer than a few minutes.

As with many mindfulness techniques, this is a practical means of visualising the outcome as a whole, taking into account the different elements. Teams are able to appreciate their part in the overall outcome and value each other's contribution. Furthermore, it makes it easier for teams to be responsive to issues and there is a culture of giving feedback swiftly so that problems *can be dealt with* at once – thus removing the fear of offering up a problem into a 'blame culture'. (It even offers a good opportunity for praise if things are going smoothly.)

Kanban

Kanban was developed by Toyota engineer Taiichi Ohno (1988) as a means of enabling all facets of a large-scale production to be aware of what was going on at all times. It has since been developed into computer software, which can be installed within the organisation.

While Kanban was developed in response to manufacturers wanting to be more responsive to customer demand, its technique can be applied to any wide-scale project.

1. Outline all the processes that the product or project needs to go through, in order – taking into account every department working on the project.

2. List the tasks.

3. State the deadline(s).

4. Instruct each team to indicate on the system (which may be a board in a communal work area or computerised software) when they are completed by writing the date of completion and ticking off the column before.

For example, it might look something like this:

By each team or person stating when their work is ready (with awareness of the deadlines), it can be pulled through by the next team. This is possible for any number of projects as long as they are all listed. Using the example above, if there are five training programmes, all five can be listed either with respective deadlines – or within one overall deadline.

What makes Kanban even more efficient is putting in 'rules' which are relevant to the process. For Toyota, if a product was found to be defective at any stage, it would be removed immediately. Using the example above, if there is a rule that (for quality purposes) only two training programmes can be evaluated at one time (e.g. there can only be a maximum of two items (or dates in this case) in the column stating 'first approval' – if there looks like there will be a backlog (as in the example where all five of the programmes have been written, but not pulled through for approval), this is something that is flagged up and someone else can be assigned temporarily to help unblock the jam. Kanban is, clearly, most efficient when everyone is aware of what needs

Implementing a new series of training programmes

1	2 Design	3 1st approval	4 Revision (if required)	5 Final approval	6 Room booking	7 Marketing	8 Delivery	9 Reflection on feedback
Task 1 completed	1.2.19 ✓	6.2.19 ✓	17.2.19 ✓	1.3.19 ✓	For 5.5.19	To start on 1.4.19		
Task 2 completed	3.2.19 ✓	7.2.19 ✓	18.2.19					
Task 3 completed	4.2.19							
Task 4 completed	5.2.19							
Task completed	6.2.19							
Final	1.3.19	14.3.19	21.3.19	25.3.19	31.3.19	1.4.19 – 10.4.19	(see room booking)	(within 3 days of delivery)

to be done – and if more than one group or one person is competent at each task.

This also enables the leader to see at a glance where patterns of issues (or performance excellence) arise. Further, because this process requires a multi-skilled team, there are always areas of development you can offer each person in each area.

Kabat Zinn (the 'founder' of mindfulness in business) has always asserted that one of the goals is to encourage others to be more mindful so that we build a more altruistic society. Bunting (2016) breaks this down further in his suggestion that mindfulness allows you to 'see worthiness in others' and to 'be compassionate' – in the workplace this allows us to see conflict less as a threat with others as obstacles to your success, but to look for root causes of the external 'problem' behaviours.

Both the systems proposed enable this visualisation of worthiness in others as well as embedding reflection and revision as a matter of course – a behaviour to be engaged in without fear of blame or repercussion.

This is not to say that the leader should not take steps to deal with consistently poor performance or areas where performance is hindered by tools or other practical matters, but, through keeping an overview of the whole picture, it enables these areas to be identified faster and any issues to be investigated and dealt with in their early stages.

Again, you will notice that meditation has not yet been proposed, and these techniques are presented as practical ways of remaining aware of, and being engaged with, the present as it happens. But what better way to enable mindfulness?

A slightly faster way to introduce such awareness comes from an exercise derived from Kanban and the scrum, known as the 'Collaboration Cycle' (Gordon *et al.,* 2018):

Try this exercise.

EXERCISE 4.1

At the start of a collaborative project, show teams the outcome and ask them to explain their role in production, for example:

In the production of a pen there may be different teams producing the cap, the shaft, the ink, the box – each with different needs and time scales. By each team explaining their role and their exacting needs, appreciation of each element and the importance of following each team's specifications and timescales is emphasised.

It is not uncommon for theatrical teams to have a 'production' meeting prior to the actors starting rehearsals to discuss timescales and needs and, sometimes, it is also essential for the actors to meet with the stage management and technical side so that both have an understanding of requirements. (It is not unheard of for actors to sometimes think themselves the centre of a project, when they may need to appreciate that without light, a stage, sound or a set, there is often no project!)

The act of making each person aware of the others' contributions goes a long way to building an understanding of their demands.

Breaking down barriers to collaboration

1. The greater good

Similar to the reasons for not sharing one's creative ideas is the fear that someone else may capitalise on an idea.

Ask yourself:

You have a lot of data on a particular topic, but you do not have the means to develop anything from your findings. A similar group has the means, but limited data. They would benefit from you sharing your work. Would you do it?

This is a common situation between medical industries, but it is slowly being broken down with the concept of 'the greater good'. The call to share cancer data (while still protecting patient confidentiality) has been increasing since 2016 when Joe Biden addressed the American Society of Clinical Oncology. Biden asked for '. . . open data, open collaboration and, above all, open minds' (Berkrot, 2016).

In emphasising the ethical need to fight for the 'greater good', individual fears of 'losing their hard work' may be reframed as a contribution to swifter overall development. It is important for the leader to recognise such contributions – the scientific and academic world does this in journals, the business world can sometimes even forget to say 'thank you'.

2. Organisations functioning as a swarm

One approach to building a collaborative structure is an organisation taking on a 'swarm' mentality. Deriving from nature, each team is aware of their own roles, but also mindful of what the rest of the organisation is doing in light of the overall goal (Panes, 2014). A further behaviour of organisational swarms is the movement to where the 'learning' is.

For example, if an organisation were to introduce a new computer system, even though not all the teams would be using it, everyone would 'down tools' and learn it and work with it so as to be familiar with it, and how their role may need to be flexible towards it. Alternatively, if a new approach is to be initiated with clients, again, all personnel – even those who do not work with clients on a regular basis – would spend time on the 'shop floor' engaging with it. This enables appreciation of what others within the organisation are doing and a time when anyone can provide feedback on how successful the initiative is and how it might be adapted.

Try this exercise.

EXERCISE 4.2

Even on a small scale, if you are introducing a new system into your team, ask the whole team to work with it and give you feedback rather than just those who would naturally access it daily. You may find that teething troubles are more quickly identified and your teams begin to have a clearer understanding of each other's contribution.

Then reflect on how well this process worked for you.

3. Organisations functioning as a pair

Some organisations insist that staff work as a pair as a matter of course – so at all times one member of staff is collaborating with another. This has an added benefit of creating a productive 'buzz' in the office. For organisations that work in this manner it has been found that:

▮ Problems are identified faster due to two pairs of eyes being aware of the job.

▮ Because staff are used to having their work checked, the fear of the 'blame culture' is removed.

▮ When a new staff member arrives, their 'on boarding' time is faster because they always have someone to ask for support.

(Timms, 2018)

Try this exercise.

EXERCISE 4.3

Next time you set a project for your team, ask them to generate the solution and work on the implementation in pairs.

Reflect on the outcomes.

The act of the swarm or allocated pairs removes the psychological barriers to collaboration but makes collaboration a natural part of the working day.

This may also have the bonus benefits of teams being able to better appreciate each other and adapt to each other's needs, improving compassion and support within the organisation overall.

Again, another mindful outcome.

4. Embrace self-selection

Try this exercise.

EXERCISE 4.4

You are writing a job description for this new organisational approach to collaborative working. However, you are not necessarily convinced that swarms or teams will work. One of the points of the job description will be that all staff work in pairs. Another is that all staff are expected to learn new initiatives.

How would you word your job description?

Often, leaders word the 'less appealing' elements of a job in an ambiguous manner, for example 'Evenings and weekends required' may be worded as 'Flexible hours required'. Or, if a job role needs 'Much of the working week spent working alone', it may be phrased as 'Requires working alone as well as within the team.'

It is often better to state a job description with the exact parameters you require, e.g. 'Six months will be spent in our Dubai office' rather than remaining ambiguous for fear of losing attractive candidates. Once those candidates find out, they may turn down the job anyway and, perhaps, have a slightly unfavourable view of your organisation.

What may be an issue for you will be not an issue for everyone and, if your organisation is clear on your parameters, then you will attract those who are willing to work under those terms. This, of course, means you have to be open minded – and brave – in taking a 'full disclosure' approach, but, again, it will attract those who will be open minded and willing to work within the culture that you have specified is important. In turn, they may also be the very people who are also compassionate and have a natural awareness of others. If you are looking to instil such a culture, the more people you can bring in who subscribe to this anyway, the faster others will engage, come round – or self-select out.

Mindful relationships

For the leader who is missing the use of a more meditative exercise, mindful meditation has also been shown – in its ability to calm the mind to bring benefits to relationships. The power of deep breathing to reduce the stress response lowers the production of cortisol, which in turn lowers the likelihood of impulsivity – beneficial for the prevention of saying or doing something which may damage a relationship unnecessarily.

While the evidence for neurological changes in the mind is limited, research has shown regular mindful meditation to:

▌ increase connectivity between the amygdala (the alarm centre) and prefrontal cortex (executive centre), which helps prevent you getting stuck in negative cycles or 'stewing' and move towards taking positive action

▌ strengthen the anterior cingulate cortex (associated with self-perception and cognitive flexibility), which again helps motivate you to make changes rather than remain within a cycle of insecurity or mistrust

▌ create change in the insula (associated with emotional awareness and empathy), making you more able to offer an open, accepting attitude towards others.

(Greenberg, 2016)

IN SUMMARY

1. Remind your teams that the main objective is achievement through collaboration. Plainly, and simply, with the collective goal as the focus, personal squabbles can be left at the door.

2. Use the Kanban Technique or the Collaboration Cycle to ensure that all facets of the team appreciate and understand the workload and pressures that they, respectively, face.

3. Utilise the scrum, Kanban or goal-related briefings to keep abreast of any issues.

4. Encourage teams to collaborate, reflect, give feedback and respond throughout the working process as a matter of course. Organisation into swarms, squads or pairs can help.

5. Potential team members who 'self-select' themselves out are not your biggest concern – be mindful of including those who mind*lessly* agree to everything.

6. Encouraging or providing the opportunity for mindful meditation with a focus on compassion can help teams become more patient and understanding (you can use the accompanying downloadable meditation).

7. Shout about your organisation's culture of mindfulness.

Should you wish to practise a meditation for compassion, please download. Go to https://www.draudreyt.com/ meditations (Password: leaderretreat).

CHAPTER 4 TOOLKIT

■ The most effective leader is the person who can harness the mind of the collective to achieve more than could be done alone.

■ Mindfulness can assist in highlighting the common goal, as well as generating a greater sense of understanding and compassion within collaborations.

Key points to remember

1. *Always* state explicitly to teams when collaboration is expected and try to find a clear means of demonstrating each team's contribution

2. *Sometimes* find an opportunity for teams to meet, even if it is a short conference call to update.

3. *Try to* see critical feedback and reflection as progressive and instil this within your teams through practice, i.e. requesting that everyone learns a new initiative and feeds back.

Take action

1. **Practise giving and receiving feedback (and teach this to your teams)**

When giving:

■ Identify the feedback criteria prior to the event.

■ Try to stick to what was observable and give evidence. It is not enough to say, 'I didn't think you did that efficiently,' without saying *why* or giving an example of what it was that made you think that.

■ Identify the elements that were competent (and better than competent!) – again, give examples of what was successful in performance.

■ Be honest – it's not about being 'funny' or getting someone to like you or asserting authority.

When receiving:

■ Retain open body language.

■ Acknowledge what you perceive as fair criticism. Do not forget you *may* ask for clarification and an example if it was not offered, e.g. 'You said I sounded abrupt – was this the case all the way through the conversation?'

■ Try not to argue – wait until they have finished before choosing to respond.

■ If nothing positive has been offered, *ask* what you did well (some people feel saying nothing means it was good).

■ *Recap the feedback in full – to check you have understood it.*

■ Thank the person, but also say which comments you have chosen not to accept (if applicable) and explain why. (This may open a helpful dialogue.)

■ Ask for advice on improvement if this has not been given.

What I tried

Date	Action

What worked for me

Date	Action

Please use a separate piece of paper if necessary.

Meditation techniques
Meditation for compassion

This is a short meditation for compassion.

To begin, take deep centring breaths – breathing in through your nose and out through your mouth. With each breath you feel calm and relaxed.

In through your nose and out through your mouth.

If any thoughts cross your mind, acknowledge them and let them pass.

If any sounds cross into your focus, acknowledge them and let them pass.

Breathe in through your nose and out through your mouth.

Picture someone you feel affection for. It can be anyone at all. Get a clear image of them in your mind and make that picture bright and vibrant.

Breathe deeply and calmly.

As you picture them, say these phrases either in your mind or out loud:

>*May you be happy*
>
>*May you be strong*
>
>*May you be free from suffering*
>
>*May you be happy*
>
>*May you be strong*
>
>*May you be free from suffering*

Once more:

>*May you be happy*
>
>*May you be strong*
>
>*May you be free from suffering*

Now picture someone whom you would like to forgive.

Even if you are not ready to forgive them completely, wishing them well means they no longer have a hold over you.

See that person in your mind and repeat:

May you be happy

May you be strong

May you be free from suffering

Again:

May you be happy

May you be strong

May you be free from suffering

Finally, see yourself as if looking in a mirror and repeat those same phrases:

May I be happy

May I be strong

May I be free from suffering

Again:

May I be happy

May I be strong

May I be free from suffering

Continue to breathe deeply and, when you are ready, become more aware of the room and open your eyes ready to get on with your day.

5 Emotional agility

The opening questions

▎ How easy is it for you to read and perceive the emotions of others?

▎ How easy is it for you to adapt your emotions?

▎ When you have adapted your emotions – are you still able to deal effectively with your original feelings?

What is emotional agility?

> *You never need to change fundamentally '. . . but the organism with the most options will yield the greatest influence'.*
>
> (Excellence Assured, 2017)

E motional agility is the ability to adapt or change your emotion in order to respond most appropriately within an interactive situation. Often, it also means that you are able to influence the situation if you have:

▎ read the situation appropriately

▎ engaged in an effective response

▎ utilised that emotion to affect the emotion of others within the interaction.

Being emotionally agile does not mean compromising yourself in any way. Its use as a skill within leadership is not in winning or losing, it is about getting things done.

It is related in part to the skill of 'emotional labour'. This is a term coined by Arlie Russell Hochschild (an American sociologist and academic) in 1983, who described it as the ability to change or adapt one's emotion to suit what is needed for the job, e.g. a frustrated teacher who is able to show compassion and patience to an angry child or a shy bailiff who is able to demonstrate assertiveness and control over an aggressive situation to get the job done. Emotional labour is part of the job itself – as essential as the technical skills required.

In leadership, emotional labour is important. Not only must you be able to complete the tasks you have, following the correct procedures as a matter of course, but, as part of negotiating, motivating, training or any interactional task, performance excellence in emotional labour can assist with generating the outcome you want.

At its very basic form, emotional agility is the ability to read the emotions of others.

Try this exercise.

EXERCISE 5.1

List as many words as you can for each of these facial expressions:

Having a wide emotional vocabulary assists with emotional agility because recognising nuances of emotion allows us to consider more options in our response. Responding to someone who you may just assume is 'happy' may be more effective if you accurately perceive them as 'anticipating' or 'proud'.

The wider our perception of human emotion, the more able we are to elicit an appropriate and effective response within ourselves.

How do I best demonstrate emotional agility?

According to author Susan David (2016), emotional agility consists of four main elements:

1. *Showing up* – facing your own thoughts and feelings and accepting them as they are.

2. *Stepping out* – being able to detach from those thoughts and feelings in order to appreciate they are just emotions and you are still in control.

3. *Walking your why* – recognising and retaining the core values which are part of you.

4. *Moving on* – the ability to make small tweaks to your mindset and habits in order to keep them in alignment with your core values. While you can accept that your values are important to you – and have been a positive influence on your successes thus far – you must not be complacent, you must always seek change and development that will improve your being.

Mindful practice will contribute to all these areas:

▎ Face your thoughts and feelings

▎ Become aware of your unconscious drives

▎ Recognise and revisit your values

▎ Keep learning, challenging and growing

Face your thoughts and feelings

It is very easy to supress negative emotions in a leadership position because you may need to do so in order to keep things moving forward. This ability to supress those emotions is, in fact, part of emotional agility and emotional labour. Despite feeling angry or upset, you are able to maintain your composure and continue a meeting or you are able to raise and impress an issue without losing your temper.

However, how you then address the real emotion when you have left the context where emotional agility has been needed will affect your ability to perform it successfully in future.

The psychodynamic approach to psychology suggests that because negative emotions are unpleasant, it is much 'easier' for the ego to engage in defence mechanisms – the thought process which suggests 'That never bothered me anyway' (Freud, 1937). However, if you are not able to properly address those emotions when the context changes, they can continue to trouble you and it may come to the point when you may behave in a 'strange' way and not realise why.

FOR EXAMPLE

Dianne has constantly suffered belittling behaviour by a superior, which frustrates and annoys her, but her supervisor is someone whom she perceives is angry (not at her, but may be taking it out on her) and, as such, she has chosen not to respond directly. Instead, she goes for a run or works out in the gym until she feels better. The next day, when she is in a better, and more assertive, frame of mind and is able to speak with the superior in a more casual context, she chooses not to address that behaviour. This behaviour happens again and again, and each time Dianne feels better after exercising and does not take the opportunity to mention anything.

Dianne gets offered another job and, in that position, another supervisor makes a careless comment, which reminds Dianne of her previous experiences. She immediately, and quite aggressively, argues back and ends up with a warning over her behaviour.

Freud would propose that Dianne was first engaging in the defences of rationalisation ('Oh, they are angry and just taking it out on me, I'll let it pass') and sublimation (channelling the emotion into sport, therefore releasing the energy in a positive manner). However, in not addressing the issue when she had the opportunity – perhaps because she thought 'it doesn't matter now' or 'I can manage it; my supervisor is the one who needs help' or even 'perhaps I misunderstood', she also repressed the initial feelings of annoyance and frustration. Unfortunately, if these emotions are not dealt with, they may be triggered unconsciously in a different context, resulting in a stronger response than Dianne would have wanted – or been able to control – because the constant repression has meant that the feelings have not 'gone away', but rather just built up – a bit like a pressure cooker. If the opportunity for slow release is not taken, explosion is often the only option.

Accepting all of your emotions – even the negative ones – and then being able to address them is part of emotional agility.

Try this exercise.

EXERCISE 5.2

Please go to the following. Go to https://www.draudreyt.com/meditations (Password: leaderretreat):

This is a meditation which takes you through a series of emotions. It asks you to consider where you are feeling those emotions, as well as reminds you that those emotions are acceptable and part of you.

This meditation is helpful in encouraging you to accept that negative feelings are ok and normal and, as such, you have the right to address them and, in enabling you to think about where you feel emotions, you will also begin to recognise when those unconscious triggers may be pulled and prevent an explosion just because of that extra awareness of how your body is feeling. The act of meditation can also help when addressing the cause of the negativity in keeping you calm and seeking resolution rather than retribution.

Other defence mechanisms are given in the Appendix at the end of this chapter.

Become aware of your unconscious drives

Try this exercise.

EXERCISE 5.3

You are allocating lifeboats on a sinking ship. Please allocate a number designating the order in which you would save the following people:[4]

A man	
A woman	
A sailor	
A doctor	
A teenager	
A baby	
A businessman	

You learn the following information about the people. Please reallocate your order, if you wish to.

A man: who is disabled	
A woman: who has mental health issues	
A sailor: who is old	
A doctor: who is homosexual	
A teenager: who is a refugee	
A baby: who is HIV positive	
A businessman: who is wealthy	

[4]This exercise is adapted from a Year 7 worksheet examining prejudice – original source unknown.

> This thought experiment can continue by adding more areas
> of hidden or more overt prejudice, for example 'Is Asian', 'Is
> divorced', 'Is a single parent', 'Is poor', 'Is a drug dealer' or 'Is
> Christian'. Each time participants are asked to reorder their
> choices, and then to reflect on why they originally prioritised
> someone, about whom – on finding something new out about
> them – they may have changed their mind.

The act of bringing some of these unconscious prejudices to
the fore – even ones where discrimination may be positive,
for example 'I would always save the baby first, because it's a
baby' – is helpful in being able to step away from habit and to
reflect actively on the thoughts that drive your behaviour.

Mindful meditation can also help in this regard and, should
you wish to engage in a meditation that is focused on
stepping outside yourself and looking down on an issue or
situation, please go to the meditation track for problem
solving.

Recognise and revisit your values

Knowing what values drive your behaviour and
remembering them on occasion so that you are not led too
far astray is also essential to continue to feel authentic.
Yacobi (2012) discusses many philosophers' approaches to
the concept of authenticity, defining it as one's true and
natural essence of self. He discusses how many factors of
the modern world can limit authenticity, in particular the
'. . . multiple identities dependent on the roles the
individual holds in society including personal,
occupational, cultural, ethnic, national, political, and
religious identities'. As with anything you practise, the
more you engage within these multiple identities, the more

your performance becomes natural and it is possible to lose sight of who you 'once were'. This can result in a very emotionally agile performance, but a nagging feeling of unhappiness or that 'something isn't right'. While Yacobi is accepting of the view that people can change over time, an element of personal constancy will, nonetheless, prevail. If this is lost – often through constant practice of the other roles played – it is possible to experience depression and a lack of satisfaction.

The practice of multiple identities is made worse by the use of social media, often deemed an essential part of your 'brand'. In posting what is 'right' for your job, it is even easier to lose sight of your authentic self, especially through becoming seduced by the 'likes' generated by the persona projected (Green, 2013).

The meditation on accepting your emotions earlier in this chapter, or any of the relaxation meditations in this book, can help you find time to recognise and accept yourself again.

Try this exercise.

EXERCISE 5.4

Chart your life on a timeline and highlight the significant moments in your life that shaped you into who you are today. Take a moment to reflect on who you were and what you thought prior to that moment and who you became after it. It may be that you can identify when you chose to take a different path or when your fundamental identity changed or grew. Recognising that difference will help remind you of elements of the authentic you, which may have become lost.

Alternatively, try this exercise.

EXERCISE 5.5

Get in contact with an old family member or friend (social media is excellent for reconnecting) and ask them the following.

From your memory of me when you knew me back then:

▮ What am I great at?

▮ What is one word that best describes me?

▮ What other people come to mind when you think of me?

Again, this can offer insight into who you were in an objective and accepting manner.

Keep learning, challenging and growing

Sometimes it can be helpful to recognise what sort of thinking holds you back. The 'Thought Analysis' exercise in the last chapter on self-care can be of help to you, but here is a reminder of the common 'unhelpful thoughts' which can hinder your ability to take action.

EXERCISE 5.6

Try to recognise your commonly used thought distortions in this list:

1. Mind reading: claiming to know someone's internal state: for example 'She just doesn't like me.'

2. Lost performative: value judgements where the person doing the judging is left out: for example 'It's bad, and everyone thinks so.'

3. Cause/effect: where cause is wrongly put outside the self: for example 'She makes me so sad.'

4. Complex equivalence: where two experiences are interpreted as being synonymous: for example 'He yelled at me, so I know he doesn't like me.'

(NLP World, 2018)

If you recognise yourself engaging in this sort of distortion, ask yourself:

▌ *Who* says? Be specific with your accusations.

▌ *Who* is 'being unfair' and in what way is this happening?

▌ *Why* else might I be feeling sad that is not related to this incident?

▌ *How* can you be sure your interpretation is correct?

These little challenges to yourself will bring a halt to your habitual thinking and enable you to reflect on your situation from a realistic point of view.

Some tips for accepting your emotions

The practice of mindfulness removes the 'dream-like habit' we tend to fall into when repeating a task we have done before – which holds as true for the performance of emotions.

▌ Before you ask for external validation, think about what you need/hope someone will say and tell it to yourself (first).

▌ Before asking for validation on your feelings, tell yourself that, no matter what, *I have the right to feel how I feel.* Once you have accepted your feelings, seek support for the *problem* (from someone you think can actually help with the *problem*).

▌ Recognise that other people have the right to feel as they feel too – even if those feelings clash with yours. Let your focus be on accepting those feelings and finding a means of collaboration, not getting them to agree with you (or it will only ever be lip service).

IN SUMMARY

1. Emotional agility is the skill of managing your emotions to enhance your social interactions.

2. Performance excellence of emotional agility is strength for any leader.

3. Emotional agility includes being able to read the emotions of others; to recognise and accept your own feelings; awareness of your unconscious drives (which may include discriminations and prejudice); awareness of your personal values; the recognition that you are always growing and learning.

4. Leaders who are adept at emotional agility need to be mindful that they are not losing sight of their own authenticity.

5. Lack of acknowledging your true feelings and using defence mechanisms may lead to behavioural changes, which are unpredictable and may be unhelpful.

6. Mindful practice helps you accept that you have the right to feel how you feel – and others do too.

CHAPTER 5 TOOLKIT

▐ Emotional agility is essential for any leadership role.

▐ To get the best out of your teams, you need to be able to recognise and respond appropriately to their emotions and, if you can be flexible with yours, you are also able to influence through this.

Key points to remember

1. *Always* work to develop your emotional agility – while you may not need everything you learn, the more options you have, the better your performance. The more people you connect with, the easier this becomes.

2. *Sometimes* see what happens when you treat others as you perceive *they* would like to be treated (even if your choice would be 'better' or 'kinder').

3. *Try to* recognise and accept your own emotions.

Take action

1. Challenge yourself

Challenge 1: ask for 360° feedback

▮ Pick three people. It can be your best friend, co-worker, peer, teammate, spouse, family, etc. Preferably, someone who knows you well.

And ask:

▮ What description comes to mind when you think of me?

▮ What is one word that best sums up how I come across to others?

Challenge 2: reach out to someone who changed your life

▮ Is there someone who you haven't seen in a while who has played a large role in your life? Or maybe there is someone you admire? Someone whose work has changed your life in some way? An actor, writer, blogger, influencer, speaker, or entrepreneur?

▮ *Call or reach out:* if you know them, pick up the phone, call them and ask to meet for coffee and a catch up and, when you do, tell them face to face what they mean to you. If you don't know them: reach out to him/her via social media. Tell them exactly how much their work has changed your life.

Challenge 3: perform one random act of kindness (without expectation of return) and reflect on how it made you feel.

What I tried

Date	Action

What worked for me

Date	Action

Please use a separate piece of paper if necessary.

Meditation techniques

Meditation to recognise where emotions rest within you

This meditation helps you to recognise and accept your feelings. Make sure you are somewhere you will not be disturbed. Switch off your phone and your computer. Sit or lie comfortably and we will begin.

Focus on your breathing – taking deep cleansing breaths – in through the nose and out through your mouth. With each exhale, allow yourself to become more and more relaxed.

Just concentrate on your breathing and, if you become distracted by a random thought or a sound, simply say 'breathe and relax' and come back to concentrating on your breathing.

Think of a time when you felt happy. Picture that time, make it clear and vibrant. Breathe and relax. As you picture that time, think about where you are feeling that sensation of happiness. Which part of your body does it start from? Can you identify where it begins? Breathe and relax. Enjoy the feelings of happiness and take a moment to recognise where in your body they feel the strongest.

Breathe and relax and slowly let that picture fade.

Focus again on breathing in through your nose and out through your mouth.

Think of a time when you felt angry – it may be with a person or about a situation. Do not picture it too clearly, but have an image in mind. Breathe and relax. Try to recognise where that feeling starts from. Where does your anger have a stem? Identify that place, breathe and relax and let that picture fade.

Breathe and relax and slowly let that picture fade.

Focus again on breathing in through your nose and out through your mouth.

Now think of a time when you felt confident – perhaps you knew you'd made the right decision, perhaps you knew things would work out, perhaps you knew exactly what you wanted. Reflect on how great the outcome was. Feel that sense of pride, success and confidence. Enjoy that sensation of pride, success and confidence. Breathe and relax. Try to recognise where that feeling starts – identify where it begins. Breathe and relax. Enjoy that sensation and acknowledge where in your body you feel it the strongest.

Breathe and relax and slowly let that picture fade.

Focus again on breathing in through your nose and out through your mouth.

Now picture a time when you felt sad. Have that image in mind. As you breathe and relax, try to recognise where in your body the strongest sensation is. Where in your body does the feeling of sadness stem from? Acknowledge it and let the picture fade.

Breathe and relax.

Focus again on breathing in through your nose and out through your mouth.

Picture a time when you felt compassion for others – perhaps for an animal or a child, even. Picture the person, animal or situation where you felt compassion. Breathe and relax. Try to recognise where that feeling of warmth stems from. That feeling that makes you want to reach out. Acknowledge that place and let the picture fade.

Breathe and relax.

Focus again on breathing in through your nose and out through your mouth.

I will now run through those emotions and I want you to recognise where in your body each of them starts. By being able to recognise where you feel your emotions, you can accept them as a part of you and also use them to guide you. The feeling of compassion may make you want to make a decision, but it is often the feeling of confidence that will make you secure in that choice. Recognising the difference between your emotions helps you gain clarity over your feelings and enables you to make clear decisions.

Breathe and relax.

Picture the time you felt happiness and recognise where that emotion starts. Acknowledge it, accept it and breathe and relax.

Breathe and relax.

Picture the time you felt anger and recognise where that emotion starts. Acknowledge it, accept it and breathe and relax.

Breathe and relax.

Picture the time you felt confidence and success and recognise where that emotion starts. Acknowledge it, accept it and breathe and relax.

Breathe and relax.

Picture the time you felt sadness and recognise where that emotion starts. Acknowledge it, accept it and breathe and relax.

Breathe and relax.

Picture the time you felt compassion and kindness and recognise where that emotion starts. Acknowledge it, accept it and breathe and relax.

Breathe and relax.

Breathe and relax.

I will count back from five and, as I do, you will become more aware of the room you are in – and you can now have better clarity over your feelings. You can remember where you acknowledged your emotions and you will, should you wish, be able to use this awareness to guide you in future.

Five, move your fingers and toes, four, move your legs and arms, three, move your head and neck, two, take a big stretch, one – when you are ready, open your eyes.

Meditation to 'look outside' the problem

This is a meditation to help you see your problems or challenges from outside. Make sure you are somewhere you will not be disturbed and switch off your phone and close your computer. Begin by breathing deeply – in through the nose, hold for a moment and out through the mouth. As you breathe naturally and deeply, allow yourself to feel more and more relaxed.

Breathe in, hold for a moment and breathe out.

Breathe in, hold for a moment, and breathe out.

Picture a big flying machine – perhaps it is an aeroplane or a zeppelin. Perhaps it is a hot air balloon, perhaps it is a bird or even a dragon. Whatever it is, picture your flying machine clearly. Fill in the colours of that flying machine so that you know it is yours. Those colours are personal to you, this flying machine is all yours.

When you have the colours clear and vibrant, climb into or onto that machine and begin your journey upwards.

Breathe in, hold for a moment and breathe out.

As you travel upwards, think about whatever has been bothering you. See it from atop your flying machine. In your own time, use your flying machine and circle it from above, travel around the problem, look at it from underneath – see if you can picture that problem from different angles, from different viewpoints. How might a bird see this problem? How might the person observing from outside see it? How can you look at it differently?

Take a moment to view that problem or challenge as an outsider, an outsider removed from being within it.

Think about where solutions can come from – how might a bird solve it? How might a person from outside suggest a solution? Look around as you fly to the many different places that a solution can come from. The whole world is at your disposal, you have many choices for your course of action – allow yourself to be open to them.

Use this time to look at that challenge from a new perspective and see if a solution can also arise from that change of view.

Remember, you can use this technique any time you want to try and step outside your challenges and look in at them as an observer. This technique allows you to see things from a different point of view, from a different perspective . . . and it can help you find a different solution.

When you are ready, begin to descend from your journey and become aware of the ground solid beneath you – it feels strong and it feels supportive. Consider how it feels as you sit or lie – you are grounded and you are supported.

Remember, you can use this flight any time you want to gain a different perspective.

When you are ready, you can open your eyes and return to the rest of your day.

Chapter 5 Appendix

Common defence mechanisms

Denial Refusing to accept a situation or fact.

Displacement While you may be angry at a partner, you may choose to channel that anger at something else, for example an umbrella that refuses to open or a child who arrives late home. This is because you have a reason for not confronting the actual source of the anger – and believe that you are angry at the displacement target fairly. (Another common example of this is 'Using X as an excuse' when 'X' is a widely acceptable reason and you feel the 'real' reason is unacceptable or you do not wish to mention it.)

Projection Rather than looking at your negative feelings, you explain a situation by saying 'They made me do it' or 'I don't like him because he doesn't like me.' You project your feelings onto another and see yours as a response.

Rationalisation Justifying a reaction in your head, for example you may have cheated on an exam but convinced yourself that 'everyone did it' or 'it was so unfair that everyone had to cheat' (notice also the use of 'everyone' as a thought distortion generalisation).

Reaction formation	Changing your reaction to hide what you feel is inappropriate, for example having a very strong reaction to someone having an affair on TV because you are actually having an affair yourself.
Repression	Pushing a painful memory away so that, eventually, you do not think about it consciously.
Sublimation	Channelling your negative energy elsewhere, for example into a sport (this can be helpful in the short term, as it allows the energy to be expelled and a calmer frame of mind to address the issue).

Inner confidence and self-esteem

The opening questions

▌ Please rate yourself in the following areas:

Self-confidence (knowledge you will succeed)

0_____10

Self-esteem (ability to like yourself, irrespective of the above)

0_____10

▌ How much is your feeling of self-esteem related to your success?

The importance of inner confidence

> *Our doubts are traitors, and make us lose the good we oft might win, by fearing to attempt.*
>
> William Shakespeare (1603), *Measure for Measure*

nfortunately, the world is one of comparison with social media making that much easier. With photographic filters and other such applications so accessible, it is no longer the established brand that can promote a favourable image, but the person next door. With leaders being ever encouraged to have a social media presence (Dottie, 2017), it is no longer possible to avoid the very 'tool' which is being linked to growing depression and anxiety (Becker *et al.,* 2012). Social media is, of course, not the only reason a leader may lack or lose confidence, but it is notable in addition to:

▐ personal issues

▐ lack of support

▐ a losing streak.

(Kanter, 2005)

Tenacity, the ability to think critically and make reasoned judgments are essential, but self-doubt at times when decisions often have to be made swiftly and without consultation can hinder performance. Therefore, confidence in your ability to do this is an asset.

Your self-confidence can be defined as the trust that you have in your abilities. It is the '. . . bridge connecting expectations and performance . . . [it] attracts investment – not just money but time, energy loyalty and commitment' (Kanter, 2005). Through life experience, and supported with mindful practice, leaders often can identify the areas in which they feel confident, along with those where this sense of competence is lower. Accurate judgement of self-confidence can help the leader to avoid reckless behaviour, but to have the courage to stand up for what they believe in. However, when a leader lacks self-confidence, this can result in being overly cautious or overly collaborative and have a detrimental effect on professional performance and standing (also discussed in Chapter 2, Problem Solving and Decision Making).

Ask yourself:

What (if any) indicators do you use to demonstrate your quality?

With self-confidence being linked to success, it is important to have a variety of success indicators to maintain a positive view of your ability. However, outside the education system, and later outside the structure of a team, the leader has no certificate to tell him or her 'well done', nor do they always have someone championing them as they would their own staff. As such, it is helpful to recognise what success looks like when it is not explicitly offered.

Try this exercise.

EXERCISE 6.1

▌ Identify what success looks like within your field. For example:

  ▌ repeat custom, recommendations or positive feedback

  ▌ bonuses or benefits

  ▌ organisational expansion

  ▌ awards or accreditations.

▌ Measure yourself against these criteria.

▌ Note areas where you are pleased and areas where you would like to improve.

▌ Identify one action in order to take a step towards that improvement.

Self-confidence is not only important for the leader in terms of your position and performance, but also for your overall well-being as well. While Chapter 8 looks at well-being as regards to resilience and longevity as a leader (notably in the eyes of others), your self-confidence also affects your self-esteem, which can influence your longevity in your own eyes.

Meshanko (2013) defines self-esteem as a mix of:

▌ being comfortable within yourself

▌ believing in yourself

▌ understanding and demonstrating your value.

Self-esteem plays a key role in the respect that a leader needs to generate in order to lead across both generation and diversity. Without respect, the leader cannot generate trust, without trust there is no loyalty from followers, without followers, there is no leadership. Meshanko (2013) found that having a healthy and realistic measure of self-esteem not only generated respect for the leader (which in turn was related to high performance), but enabled the leader to give respect, which was a fundamental element within high-performing teams.

It is noted that self-esteem is a measure of how much you like yourself and self-confidence a measure of your success. While the two do not need to sit hand-in-hand, they are often linked. The more you recognise an achievement, the greater your self-esteem. Or at least, regardless of personal nature, a win for your self-confidence is an easy boost for your self-esteem and a knock to the former often has a negative effect on the latter

With a healthy regard for both self-confidence and self-esteem central to leadership performance, it is helpful for the leader to keep them buoyant.

Try this exercise.

EXERCISE 6.2

Identify a situation when you felt and behaved confidently.

How do you feel physically when you think of that situation?

Can you identify the sensations and feelings in your body and where they manifest?

Write down one sentence that sums up the situation or the outcome, for example 'I realise I am stronger than I thought I was', 'I had to do it on my own and I did' or 'I knew I was right and stood up for myself.'

Remind yourself of that situation the next time you feel like your confidence is lacking.

Alternatively, try this.

EXERCISE 6.3

List the wins in your life:

Aged 0–12	Teenage years/ early 20s	Recently	Those I am aiming for in the next 5 years

This exercise reminds you that you have succeeded in the past (and may even remind you of a time where you displayed skills you had forgotten about)[5] and encourages you to think towards future successes.

---
[5]When doing this exercise with a client, she was reminded of negotiating a lead role in a school play at eight years old – she had forgotten she had the confidence to attempt something so 'cheeky' that her teacher had 'had a word' with her mother.

Smith (2014) reviewed research into mindfulness and confidence, finding that those who practised mindfulness were better able to separate when a failure came from within or from something outside the person's control. This, in turn, had a positive effect on self-esteem ratings as well as the type of language that people used to describe and speak to themselves. Smith found that with mindful practice 'self-criticism' became more constructive, and reflection following failure more compassionate.

The importance of self-esteem

> *This above all;*
>
> *To thine own self be true.*
>
> William Shakespeare (1602), *Hamlet*

Although work on self-confidence can support a healthy self-esteem, it is also important for the leader – especially one who is already compassionate (see also chapter on Self-Care) to work on maintaining self-esteem outside its link to confidence to avoid any 'rescuer' tendencies which can be detrimental to leadership relationships.

The concept of the rescuer was identified by Karpman (1967) who discussed its appearance along with the other two identities which make up the 'Karpman Drama Triangle'.

The three roles are strategies (or behaviours) which intertwine, and enable the person 'playing' them to avoid dealing with the real issues that may be troubling them.

- The *victim* feels powerless and at the mercy of events.

- The *persecutor* looks to blame or punish and may behave in a strict, authoritarian and, perhaps, abusive manner.

- The *rescuer* seeks a *victim* in order to be able to jump in and 'fix' the problem (and may create or even fabricate a *persecutor* (who may be an entity such as 'the organisation' as well as a person).

According to Levin (2016), the leader is not exempt from falling into these roles – with the compassionate leader most at risk to play the part of the rescuer.

According to psychodynamic theory, the *rescuer* is someone who is often seeking a corrective experience. This may be because they have lacked the affection they desired in childhood and are looking to fill this gap through offering that love and compassion they were missing to others. Such people often are drawn to the care professions or roles in which they can offer support to others (Riley, 2010). This is because they have found a boost to their self-esteem when they are needed. While not every person who is a compassionate leader is looking to 'rescue' those with lowered self-esteem due to a lack of affection, they may channel that need into others, mistakenly believing that, if they can 'fix' someone else, they themselves will be fixed.

Unfortunately, this is not the case and can result in the leader disempowering their team by making them over-reliant on the leader and, in turn, this can add extra emotional pressure to an already demanding role.

Try this exercise.

EXERCISE 6.4

If you find yourself being drawn into being overly understanding towards a specific person, first ask yourself:

▌ What is it in that person that I am drawn to? (Often, the rescuer sees themselves or a familiar situation in the person they are trying to rescue.)

▌ Am I actually helping empower them if I am solving their problems for them?

Then practise asking coaching questions, for example:

▌ What support would you like me to offer?

▌ How do you think the organisation can best help you?

(Further coaching questions can be found at the end of this chapter.)

Or signpost them to teams within the organisation that can offer support:

Useful numbers:
Within my organisation:
Outside my organisation:

In order to build your own self-esteem try the following:

▌ **Accept compliments and compliment yourself.** Practise giving genuine compliments, unprompted, and accepting them graciously.

▌ **Use criticism as a learning experience.** Everybody sees the world differently, from their own perspective. What works for one person may not work for another. Criticism is just the opinion of somebody else. Be assertive when receiving criticism, do not reply in a defensive way or let criticism lower your self-esteem.

▌ **Try to stay generally cheerful and have a positive outlook on life.** Only complain or criticise when necessary and, when you do, do so in a constructive way. Offer others (true) compliments and congratulate them on their successes – you are *not* on the same journey!

▌ **Give yourself the best chance.** Work effectively, prepare. If in doubt, *ask* for help – and ask the right people . . . friends are *not* always the most useful!

IN SUMMARY

1. While self-confidence and self-esteem are different entities, they can be linked in positive and detrimental ways. The leader needs a healthy balance of both.

2. Being able to identify the success criteria within your field can help you acknowledge your 'wins'. This is particularly useful when you are otherwise feeling down or as if you are on 'a losing streak'. Mindful practice helps you separate a failure which was within your control from one outside it.

3. Self-confidence and self-esteem within a leader helps them offer and generate respect. Respect has been shown to influence performance.

4. The person drawn to caring professions or supportive roles may be doing so due to recognising a lack of something (usually affection) within themselves. In seeking a 'corrective experience', they may fall into 'rescuer' behaviours, which inhibit their teams rather than empower them.

5. Coaching questions and signposting can help you, habitually, empower your teams, as can a focus on building up your own self-esteem.

CHAPTER 6 TOOLKIT

▍ Leaders need to be able to respond positively to the emotional demands that the current business world brings.

▍ You are much more connected with your teams, and progression often depends on forming relationships or collaborations with others that may be short or long term.

▍ It is essential to retain your self-confidence and self-esteem within this constantly demanding and changing environment.

Key points to remember

1. *Always* maintain a healthy attitude to others – respect them and the differences between you.

2. *Sometimes* remind yourself of your recent 'wins' as well as the values which you like about yourself.

3. *Try to* do point 2, even when you are feeling down.

Take action

1. **Remind yourself of your key values**

- Recognise and praise yourself when you demonstrate them.

2. **Start a list of useful numbers and websites[6] which you can call on for help or to which you can signpost others, for example:**

- Acas www.acas.org.uk (visit the 'contact us' page).

- Citizen's Advice Bureau www.citizensadvice.org.uk/ (UK), tel: 0344 488 9629.

- Mind www.mind.org.uk (visit 'information and support' page).

- Other numbers

3. **Practise coaching questions**

Example coaching questions include:

- What is happening in the current situation? (Specify names.)

- What have you tried that has worked in the past?

- How might X view the situation?

- Who might be able to offer you help?

- What do you see as a positive outcome?

- Identify three possible actions – which might be the most successful?

- What have you considered doing?

---

[6]Correct at the time of writing.

What I tried

Date	Action

What worked for me

Date	Action

Please use a separate piece of paper if necessary.

2 part

Personal applications

Self-care

7

The opening questions

▍ Do you believe in self-care?

▍ Are you ok with slowing down?

▍ Do you recognise when you need to slow down?

Why is self-care essential for the successful leader?

> *Almost everything will work again if you unplug it for*
> *a few minutes, including you.*
>
> TED speaker, Anne Lamott, 2018

The start of this book has looked at the applications of mindfulness to enhance overt leadership skills and team performance. It is now important to spend a short time looking within the self. As you will have recognised, especially in the last chapter on inner-confidence and self-esteem, longevity in leadership is as reliant on the personal strengths of the leader as on what you deliver.

If a leader does not take time to engage in self-care, their performance will suffer.

Busy people who multi-task, particularly in leadership positions, are no longer offering the best, nor healthiest, practice if they work consistently on auto-pilot. They can lose attention to detail, miss opportunities and burn out personally and professionally.

However, if the world around you is not going to slow down, you will need to find a way to manage. Therefore, countering your potential for overload is essential.

This is especially true if you are already an emotionally agile leader. Practising mindfulness brings a number of emotional healing methods to the leader who is adept at emotional labour – the adaptation of one's external performance to elicit behaviour in others, for example the leader who remains calm in a crisis because s/he does not want to agitate the team.

However, it is notable that this is one of the benefits of mindful practice often overlooked in texts on the subject. As such, the next three chapters focus on how mindfulness can assist with strengthening the already emotionally agile professional as they take on the position of carer or container of the anxieties of their team. The importance of this section is that the caretaker is also often reluctant to realise they may need care and, as such, not let others care for him or her (Lisansky Beck 2016) – this is, of course, unsustainable.

With mindfulness simply making you more aware of your current habits, consider whether you set any time aside to look after yourself.

Try these exercises, which form a self-care audit (adapted from Markway, *Psychology Today,* 2015).

EXERCISE 7.1

General self-care

▌ Do you understand the difference between self-care and self-indulgence?

▌ Do you believe that self-care shows weakness?

The most common critics of mindfulness and mindful practice would answer 'no' to both these questions. Many dismiss self-care as 'self-indulgent' or 'wallowing' instead of 'just getting on with things' – and they are the same critics who say mindfulness encourages such behaviour because of its focus on looking inwards (Rudgard, 2017, citing Dr Anne Grey, chair of spirituality of the Royal College of Psychiatrists). However, Dr Grey makes it clear that it is merely a warning to practise mindfulness in a context where support and an understanding of the process can be sought. Becoming more self-aware can be a frightening process, as you may recognise negative behaviours or emotions that previously were repressed and hidden. However, having support or techniques to help you work through them enables you to move on with your life without such hindrance.

EXERCISE 7.2

Interpersonal self-care

▐ Do you have a small group of people you can call on for support?

▐ Do you nurture relationships with people who make you feel good about yourself?

▐ Are you able to set appropriate boundaries in your relationships?

If you have been able to answer 'yes' to the above questions, this is a good foundation for knowing you have support when facing stress or emotionally charged situations. Social support is a huge contributor to the reduction of stress, whether your network is there to offer practical help, a distraction or merely to listen and allow you to talk.

Leaders, especially, need support because their role is often lonely as they stand out in front of the pack. While you may be unable to burden your team, be aware of who you can speak to when you are troubled (e.g. colleagues, coaches or other professionals), otherwise it becomes very hard for you to function effectively.

Here is a simple reminder to be mindful – if you are continually containing the anxieties of others (like a sponge mops up water), unless you take a moment to squeeze it (i.e. care for yourself), the sponge will no longer be able to function as a sponge. In order to continue functioning well as a leader, you need to engage in some self-care.

EXERCISE 7.3

Physical self-care

▍ How many times a week do you exercise?

▍ Do you generally nourish your body with food that is good for you?

▍ Do you feel comfortable in your own body?

▍ Do you *sleep* and rest when you're tired?

▍ Do you unwind before bedtime so that you can sleep better?

▍ Do you get outside each day?

If you do not take time to look after your body, your body will force you to make time by falling sick. As much as leaders like to think they are indestructible, they are also human. This means your physical body is susceptible not just to stress, but to disorders in general – more so if you do not look after it. The busy executive who is always entertaining clients to rich food and drink or skipping meals in order to get things done, staying up late to connect across the world or to finish the day's workload eventually will burn out. If the reason you are doing all this work is because you believe you are the best person to do it, then you have an incentive to maintain your body so that you can keep going for longer.

Here are three simple tips to quickly improve your physical health:

1. Get out anyway!

The fresh air always does us good – and, even if you aren't regular with your morning run, consider venturing out for a walk at lunchtime or perhaps in the evening or weekends with friends and family.

2. Brighten your laptop with a sunny screensaver

Pictures of a beautiful place or sunny climate offer us a mini snapshot into happy times and memories. This can generate a sense of warmth and relaxation even with wind beating at the door. Moore (2015, cited by Tang, 2018) reminds us that, as visual creatures, you are often quickly moved by imagery and having photos of places you love (with the ensuing memories of people we love attached) can reinforce those feelings of affection as well.

3. Keep evergreens

Not only does pine smell lovely, but researchers at Kyoto University in Japan found that healthy volunteers who strolled through a pine forest for 15 minutes a day reported more positive ratings on a mood scale compared with those who did not. Furthermore, Pycnogenol, derived from pine, has been found to ease jet lag as well as '. . . circulatory problems, knee pain and menstrual cramps; it may even improve memory in the elderly' (Altshul, 2012).

EXERCISE 7.4

Mental self-care

▍ Do you regularly stimulate your *brain* through learning new things?

▍ Do you have an outlet for your *creativity*?

The role of the leader is about moving your organisation forward, growth and development. If you do not take the time to do this for yourself, you will find that you will fall behind.

EXERCISE 7.5

Financial self-care?

▍ Do you know what your day-to-day spending is?

▍ Do you over-indulge or splurge financially and feel guilty afterwards?

Finance is an area of self-care that previously has been overlooked. It is wise for the leader, who may manage a budget, to be aware of their personal spending habits in case negative patterns played out at home are mirrored in the workplace.

These questions are there to make you think about your own personal habits – and, once you are aware of them, you have the option to make changes. It is notable that interpersonal, mental, physical and financial health are contributors to positive overall well-being – and, in turn, performance.

As highlighted earlier, some leaders – and indeed the sceptics – see self-care as 'unnecessary' and, by association, mindfulness as 'selfish'. They prefer to 'keep giving', sometimes believing that it is essential to 'put others first'. However, this approach can be misplaced. It is wise to take a moment to consider the aeroplane safety instruction 'affix your own mask first'. If you are not physically, emotionally and mentally healthy, at best you will not help others successfully, at worst you will contribute to the problem. No one would dive into an underwater rescue if they could not swim, so why would you offer your services when you may need to break promises or let others down because you are not emotionally fit yourself?

In Chapter 6 you were asked to consider if your compassion as a leader was due to the need to 'rescue'. Such leaders who have a desire to 'fix' things, can disempower their teams, yet 'rescuing' behaviour often is stubbornly dismissed by those who demonstrate it as 'just trying to be helpful'.

Try this exercise.

EXERCISE 7.5[7]

Melanie comes to see you, as she has just gone through a break up and she is struggling to cope.

Melanie says she is really unhappy with the help she has received from her friends, no one seems to understand, they are all siding with her partner and say she is causing problems for the children.

Melanie wants to work, but she knows she is emotional and is worried about her performance.

---

[7] Exercise adapted from Helplines.org Training: https://helplines.org/

Which is the closest to your response?

▌**Response 1** Straight away, you provide general information about divorce and how it could affect Melanie. You also inform Melanie that there are good legal advisors in the area who could handle the matter, and tell her that she needs to speak to the school and see what they can do to help with the children. Meanwhile, you tell Melanie to speak to her line manager to arrange a meeting so Melanie can arrange time off should this be necessary, and you give her the 'cover' procedure.

▌**Response 2** You might ask a little more about her circumstances and check what Melanie wants to do in terms of keeping her working hours/workload while being able to manage her personal life. You tell her to speak to you at the end of the day with her proposals if she hadn't thought about it right now. You give Melanie the details of the Well-being team, in case she needs them, and tell her that support groups can sometimes be helpful and you will ask well-being about signposting her. Finally, you ask Melanie what support – outside those she mentions – she has, and when she may be able to approach them.

▌**Response 3** It happens that Melanie's situation is very similar to yours – your brother was going through the same, and his workplace was terribly unsupportive. Because of this, you want Melanie to know that, if she needs anything, you are happy to help. You tell Melanie that it can get acrimonious and give her the number of your brother's lawyer who, in the end, handled things really well. You ask her if it's ok if you ring the Well-being team on her behalf, and do so there and then if she agrees. You then tell her to take whatever time she needs and that you will personally cover her work.

While each response may hold some elements of truth, please consider the one closest to your natural instincts.

▎ If you chose response 1, your approach is 'problem solving'.

▎ If you chose response 2, your approach is 'facilitating'.

▎ If you chose response 3, your approach is 'rescuing'.

Response 1 is informative, but may come across as slightly cold – or meaningless. Simply taking the time to find out what Melanie suggests may make a difference in the solutions you are able to offer. However, response 1 still demonstrates that you know what is available and allows Melanie to seek her own support.

Response 2 is as informative, and may be more meaningful because of the time taken to find out a little more about the situation prior to making recommendations. Furthermore, it can be helpful because, while you may have a solution in mind, Melanie too may have a preference and, rather than pre-empting, you are then (if it is workable) able to follow her lead. Suggestions from within the 'other' are also more likely to be executed compared to those which have been imposed. Further, the act of finding out more information and what Melanie wishes to do removes your personal emotion, reaction and judgement, which can be helpful to you – especially if the situation triggers something personal within you. A facilitating approach is a reminder that everyone responds differently and, as long as the workplace goal is achieved, there is no need for further analysis.

Response 3 is most common to the overly compassionate leader – it is the approach of the 'rescuer'. The 'rescuer' is often someone who has experienced their own adversity and either lessens their own pain through helping others or wants to 'save' others from experiencing what they went through. It is particularly common in leaders within caring professions (e.g. education and health (Tang, 2015)) because often they are drawn there, seeking a 'corrective experience', i.e. some purpose to make their own hardship seem better.

So is compassion a weakness?

Absolutely not!

On the face of it, there is nothing wrong with showing such a high level of compassion until you look at it within the context of leadership – and ask:

1. Would you be able to do the same for your *entire* team?
2. How does making that person dependent upon your help, help *them*?
3. What if you have misunderstood the situation and your help is misplaced?
4. Will this level of compassion (if you then had to demonstrate it to more people in your team who may all go through something similar) be possible to sustain – while maintaining performance excellence in your job?

Making it easier to say 'no'

As well as developing the coaching skills suggested in Chapter 6 and being aware of where you can signpost your teams, mindful thinking will make you more aware of your personal reasons for needing to indulge others.

Common reasons you may be reluctant to say no include:

▌ feeling guilty

▌ enjoyment of 'being needed'

▌ feeling that you are valued or worthy because you are needed

▎having a reputation of 'That's so-and-so; s/he'll always be able to help'

▎not knowing what to say.

Some tips to help you help others help themselves

Sometimes having a helpful, yet empowering, response preprepared can help you when you are caught *off-guard* in a 'please help me' situation.

Practice this:

1. Of course I can help, but I can only do it at X time.

2. I only have five minutes, then I must get on with X.

3. Can I let you know at the end of the day/tomorrow?

4. Here's one I made earlier (give them a sample template).

5. How would you like me to help you?/What do you think is best for me to do?/What would be of most help to you at this time?

The first three also relate to another mindful moment – remind yourself never to say 'yes' when you are in a good mood.

While a concern with the first three statements is sometimes '. . . but they will stop asking me', you may need to ask yourself – is this really a bad thing?

With regards to points 4 and 5, these will take some preparation, but will, ultimately, save you a lot of time and energy. Having a template pre-prepared, especially for things which you are commonly asked, means that you can offer someone support without having to take the time to go through something step by step – and you are also encouraging them to take on the work themselves – with guidance.

Similarly, point 5 requires you to know what is in your remit to offer – so always familiarise yourself with the emotional support you are able to signpost someone to – and then empower them by asking what they feel would be best in terms of your role in helping them.

So that's them, what about me?

Once you are more adept at facilitating others to find their own solutions, it is also helpful to take time for yourself. This is again where mindful meditation – often with a focus on self-esteem – can help you. People who are drawn to offer over and above the amount of help really required often have issues with their self-esteem, and meditation with a focus on self-value has been shown to improve self-worth and self-compassion (Smith, 2014).

Try this exercise.

EXERCISE 7.6

If you have 10 minutes available, download the track for the mindful meditation focused on self-value, which also includes positive affirmations for self-worth. It is available at https://www.draudreyt.com/meditations. (Password: leaderretreat).

Alternatively, if you do not have much time, try this exercise.

EXERCISE 7.7

Write down three things you value about yourself

Think of these things as part of what got you your position and, if you would charge highly for your services in the workplace, remember that your emotional skills are as valuable – even if their financial worth is not so clearly defined.

Self-care for your team

As well as the internal benefits of mindfulness, such as emotional flexibility, greater acceptance and compassion, there are practical suggestions for building in self-care specific routines into daily practice, such as reminding your teams to:

▌ take breaks to go to the bathroom and hydrate as needed

▌ stand up more and move around every hour as well as to turn off all electronic devices for a set time

▌ experience the benefits of going out for lunch and sessions on mindful eating

▌ include items that promote mindful moments including photos, cartoons, quotes – and sharing them

▌ (if possible) listen to mindful or soothing music.

It is sometimes helpful to think about self-care as the foundations which keep a boat afloat – as other pressures keep pressing down on it or knocking it from side to side.

Try this exercise.

EXERCISE 7.8

Which of these do you currently look after?

▌ Hygiene and appearance

▌ Sleep and relaxation

▌ Healthy leisure

▌ Healthy eating habits

▌ Exercise

▌ Inner peace and spirituality

▌ Self-improvement

▌ Sobriety

▌ Health management

Identify an area that comes out short and write down one
thing you will do to make an improvement in that area:

_____

_____

_____

_____

And finally . . .

Remind yourself of who you are and what is important
to you.

EXERCISE 7.9

Empty your pocket, bag or purse and identify something that
you regularly keep in there. Take a moment to remind yourself
why you carry it and why it is so important.

It is always important to remember your worth as an
individual because that, in turn, will remind you to care for
yourself as well as others.

IN SUMMARY

1. Sceptics may believe that self-care is selfish or unnecessary.

2. The more emotionally compassionate a leader you are, the more likely you are to fall into being a 'rescuer', which can be unhelpful to those you are trying to support.

3. It is possible to prepare and practise statements or have items you can use to help empower others rather than 'doing it for them'.

4. Mindful meditation and affirmations can build self-worth, self-value and self-esteem by reminding you of each.

5. It is possible to enhance the self-care of your teams through practical intervention, such as reminding them to take bathroom breaks.

6. Remind yourself of your individuality – and hopefully your impact and meaning as such – through looking at something you carry which is meaningful to you from time to time.

CHAPTER 7 TOOLKIT

▮ Self-care is not often discussed within leadership, and it is often approached with the same scepticism as mindfulness. Yet, with the demands growing on the leader – especially one who is emotionally agile – refusing to pay attention to self-care has performance repercussions.

▮ Self-care is essential, not selfish or self-indulgent.

Key points to remember

1. *Always* make time to look after yourself – including formal methods, for example seeing a mentor; and informal ones, for example switching your phone off while having lunch.

2. *Sometimes* make a point of modelling this behaviour explicitly for your team – make them aware it is ok to take a moment for themselves when they need to.

3. *Try to* recognise when you are engaging in unhealthy behaviours, for example working very late. Identify the reason and try to put a stop to it.

Take action

1. **Practise 'boundary setting' phrases**

■ How would you suggest I can best support you?

■ What would you like to do and how can I help with that?

■ I will let you know on [later date].

■ Who else can support you?

. . . and behaviours

■ Set 'office hours' and stick to them.

■ Do not answer the phone or engage in anything work-related after a certain time.

■ Concentrate on one thing at a time (e.g. put your phone away when in a meeting).

■ Have templates/procedures/answers prepared for common questions – ready to give out rather than having to explain it all (again!).

Engage in informal self-care/moments for yourself:

■ Make sure you go to the toilet when you need to!

■ Take a proper lunchbreak – even if it is short – step away from your desk physically.

■ Take a moment to listen to the birds or enjoy the warmth of the sun when you are driving or commuting somewhere.

■ When you engage in a task – even a simple one such as taking your jacket off – think about it mindfully – break down and recognise every little thing you are doing – just for those seconds you are doing it.

2. **Try some formal self-care for your workplace**

- Make sure that your team also know where to signpost their own staff – perhaps add a well-being page to the organisational intranet.

- Find out about the well-being events on offer within your organisation and organise a team session to attend.

- At the next 'team day' consider a well-being activity, for example yoga, singing/playing music together, a massage session.

- Encourage your team (if possible) to have personal effects near them so that they can get a 'hit' of oxytocin (the bonding hormone) as they see them.

What I tried

Date	Action

What worked for me

Date	Action

Please use a separate piece of paper if necessary.

Meditation techniques
Meditation for self-value

This is a short meditation to reaffirm your value.

Find a quiet place where you will not be disturbed and switch off from the world. This is your time.

Begin by taking three deep centring breaths.
Breathe in through your nose, hold for two.
Out through your mouth four, three, two, one.

Breathe in through your nose, hold for two.
Out through your mouth four, three, two, one.

Breathe in through your nose, hold for two.
Out through your mouth four, three, two, one.

And as you breathe, recite the following affirmations:

- I am a worthy person.
- I am a good person.
- My thoughts and ideas are valuable.
- I can be even more successful than I am now.
- My skills are helpful.
- I make a difference to the world.
- I deserve the good things that will happen to me and I am ready to receive them.

Breathe in through your nose, hold for two.
Out through your mouth four, three, two, one.

- I am a worthy person.
- I am a good person.
- My thoughts and ideas are valuable.
- I can be even more successful than I am now.

▌ My skills are helpful.

▌ I make a difference to the world.

▌ I deserve the good things that will happen to me and I am ready to receive them.

Breathe in through your nose, hold for two.
Out through your mouth four, three, two, one.

▌ I am a worthy person.

▌ I am a good person.

▌ My thoughts and ideas are valuable.

▌ I can be even more successful than I am now.

▌ My skills are helpful.

▌ I make a difference to the world.

▌ I deserve the good things that will happen to me and I am ready to receive them.

Repeat all or some of those affirmations whenever you need to.

Breathe in through your nose, hold for two.
Out through your mouth four, three, two, one.

Breathe in through your nose, hold for two.
Out through your mouth four, three, two, one.

Breathe in through your nose, hold for two.
Out through your mouth four, three, two, one.

When you are ready, open your eyes and come back to the room.

Emotional resilience and well-being

The opening questions

▌ What does 'emotional resilience' mean to you?

▌ What is your response to failure?

▌ Do you think you are currently coping with all the demands on your time?

The world won't slow down, but you can

The world continues to speed up. Timms (2018) offers a reminder that knowledge that once served for hundreds of years is now becoming obsolete faster. If you learned a new skill in the 1800s, that knowledge still would have been relevant by 1900, but learning a new skill in 2018 means you may be learning one that supersedes it within months. Not only that, but technology has enabled multi-tasking and it is now expected of everyone, and leaders in particular, that you can manage a number of things at once. This may include keeping yourself up to date within your role, your industry and also considering your future development *while* maintaining an equally fast-paced personal life. Furthermore, the speed at which it is possible to gain access to information, to things you want to purchase, learn or even people whom you might date means you now have to actively remind yourself that you can stop should you need – or wish – to, but it is more commonly expected of you to do it all – and do it all quickly.

Perhaps a cultural shift really is needed. Perhaps everyone just needs to slow down. But until society enables a change in tempo, multi-tasking, gaps between expectation and reality and a steadfast need to keep going nonetheless remain the norm. The leader who can manage this – and maintain their quality of performance is the most effective.

The quote at the start of this chapter is used for two reasons:

1. There is a societal expectation that it is good to pick oneself up and keep going.

2. Sometimes, even though the route is tougher to navigate, you need to take it, and it is awareness, and nurturing, of your emotional resilience and personal well-being that will sustain you.

Why build emotional resilience and well-being?

> *Hard driving and strategic leaders can become even more effective as they identify their own suffering, accept those feelings, focus on ways to ease – versus deny – their suffering and related feelings and then generalise this awareness into compassionate*

> *interactions with those working for them. This evolved*
> *state of leadership should strengthen their*
> *abilities . . . to manage the demands of 21st century*
> *business dynamics.*
>
> Wasylyshyn and Masterpasqua, 2018

In the last chapter, the importance of self-care for physical, mental and emotional health – and longevity as a leader – was emphasised. This chapter encourages you to explore two linked areas – emotional resilience and overall well-being. Again, exactly as the quote suggests, these personal skills are essential for the 'evolved' leader in the current business world.

Emotional resilience may be defined as the ability of an individual to adapt to or withstand situations of stress and adversity. An emotionally resilient leader can manage their emotional reactions within a crisis, enabling them to navigate their way through; they are able to spring back from failure. While there is some research evidence suggesting this is partly inborn, it can be learned, although often it means beginning with a challenging self-reflection.

Well-being may be defined as '. . . the state of being healthy and happy' (Cambridge Online Dictionary, 2018). Yet, well-being in the workplace is an ongoing contemporary issue. There are a growing number of well-being related sickness days being taken (HSE, 2016) and it was reported widely in 2015 that stress was not seen as an acceptable reason to take time off work (with only 19 per cent saying that it was) (White, 2015). However, lack of attention to your well-being may result in an inability to work effectively – no matter what your views on taking sick days.

Building emotional resilience and focusing on your well-being is a part of your self-care routine, but these two elements merit a chapter to themselves because they (along with acceptance of limitations in the following chapter) involve posing a challenge to previous beliefs and practices, which can be much harder to beat. Emotional resilience requires you to overcome adversity and well-being to maintain that healthy mindset.

Emotional discord is commonly caused by a gap between expectation and reality (Baucells and Sarin, 2011). When expectations are raised so high that reality cannot catch up, disappointment – and sometimes even depression – ensues. This is a growing phenomenon within the younger executives joining organisations who have grown up on the 'you can do anything' mentality, within an economy which (at the time of writing) is ever worsening (Burkeman, 2013). However, you may hold some unhelpful concepts, too.

Try this exercise.

EXERCISE 8.1

What myths prevail in your thought process?

▌ Will your prince(ess) come and will you live 'happily ever after'?

▌ Is the world ultimately 'fair'?

The concerns with the 'Disneyfication' of fairy tales – tales which originally were passed down as metaphors on the dangers of 'modern' life – often are addressed. Young couples are now warned against the 'happily ever after' (without clear communication and a unification of goals). So too now is the psychological fallout from giving all children a medal rather than setting out the idea at a young age that:

▌ there will be competition

▌ those who succeed demonstrate talent or hard work – often both

▌ that it is possible to fail, but to then try again and succeed.

If one has not learned that failure is an option – and a learning experience, as disappointments build – what can result is engagement in 'blocking' behaviours to avoid dealing with them, such as:

▌ addictive behaviours, including drug and alcohol misuse

▌ excessive worrying or talking – without taking action

▌ restlessness and an inability to 'stop'

▌ denial, anger or irritability.

Or 'drowning' behaviours, such as:

▌ exhaustion and burnout

▌ depression

▌ catastrophising

▌ withdrawal

(Burch, 2008)

The more you are able to acknowledge and understand your difficult thoughts and emotions, which arise most swiftly from setbacks, the less likely you are to elicit these unproductive behaviours.

Building emotional resilience

A recent study cited in Mindful.org found that people who practised mindfulness '. . . can better cope with difficult thoughts and emotions without becoming overwhelmed' (Mindful.org, 2016). One of the practices identified was the repetition of positive, healing affirmations while also engaging in relaxation, meditation, breathing or yoga activities. These affirmations included:

▌ May I be kind to myself.

▌ May I find peace and healing.

▌ I am doing the best that I can in this moment.

▌ May I find ease with things just as they are.

The practice of affirmations is common to meditation and yoga and is explained to the satisfaction of the scientific mind by Richard Wiseman in his book, *The Luck Factor* (2003). Wiseman said that people are 'naive empiricists', which means that it is human nature to look for coincidences, things which support the perspective of the world being held at that time. As such, through using positive affirmations such as 'I am a lucky person', the mind is primed to look for positive (or 'lucky') occurrences.

For instance, look at the following exercise.

EXERCISE 8.2

Repeat the following phrase three times: 'I am able to cope effortlessly with the challenges of the day' and the naïve empiricist will be inclined to draw your attention, albeit unconsciously, to examples of when that phrase was true.

Wiseman found that he was able to change the perceived fortunes of self-labelled 'unlucky' people to 'luckier' ones through repeating, 'I am a lucky person and today is going to be another lucky day' each morning. It is worth seeing if the same will work for you.

Focusing on reality does not mean a final farewell to pleasant childhood myths, but rather an ability to appreciate them for what they are – perceptions of a concept rather than common examples.

While also challenging, emotional resilience can be built through the recognition that failure happens, but it is something to be learned from.

Accepting failure is an option – and an opportunity to learn

However, 'failure' can come at a price for successful executives and it is often reframed, repressed and then deleted. However, working mindfully with failure, that is reviewing failure and embracing it as a lesson learned (rather than writing it off with a platitude), is a very powerful tool for future success. It is also a point of sweet comparison. Therefore, the ability to reflect not just on the failure, but the reactions surrounding it, can offer insights into both problem solving and team coherence.

Try this exercise.

EXERCISE 8.3

Next time you are faced with a failure instead of focusing on why your strengths were unsuccessful, look at the person or the situation that did achieve and ask:

▌ What do I need to develop to achieve that result?

CASE STUDY

Reflect

A client approached an agency with regards to applying for a job. The agency responded that he '. . . was not suitable'. The client immediately tried to prove why he thought he would be appropriate – protestations which the agency dismissed. The client was left feeling disappointed that he could not argue his case.

In working with this client, he realised that, if he accepted the answer, the questions he could have asked were growth ones:

▌ What skills do I need to develop for the post?

> ▌ What specific requirements of the post will I need to make me more suitable?
>
> Instead, what had happened was a stalemate with the agency perceiving him as 'difficult' and the client feeling worse than simply being rejected.

It is also worth recognising that, sometimes, failure can be perceived wrongly.

As with the case study, leaders are very familiar with volatile settings, but sometimes your successes are not recognised; sometimes rewards are received long after the act was performed; sometimes what seemed likely turns out not to be so – or vice versa. Therefore, it is essential to nurture a form of resilience which can be self-generated without any other more universal or tangible success indicators, for example certificates or prizes. A deeper understanding of organisation-specific rewards or field-specific success criteria can build mental toughness in executives (Clough and Strycharczyk, 2012). This also builds a feeling of confidence in the self because the results are defined – rather than a reliance on a confirmation from 'superiors' or colleagues.

Try this exercise.

EXERCISE 8.4

▌ Identify the success criteria in your field (you can look back to what you identified in Chapter 6).

▌ Ask your team to identify what they believe to be success criteria in your field.

▌ Make this identification explicit.

Not that making this 'explicit' does not mean turning it into a target, or something to indicate performance, but the clarity that this exercise affords will instil a confidence within your team that they can recognise when they are on the right track.

'Anyone can win a good hand, the secret is playing a bad hand to best effect.'
(anon)

Resilience is also about bouncing back after failure, and failure is nothing to be ashamed of. As poker players will say, it's easy to win when the cards are in your favour, but the skill lies in playing a bad hand well.

One method of challenging negative thinking, which may creep in after a setback, is to practise an empowering thought process.

This involves a brief understanding of the categories of unhelpful or negative thoughts:

▊ *Predicting the future,* for example: 'I'm going to a party and I know no one will talk to me.'

▊ *Jumping to conclusions or mind reading,* for example: 'They're all laughing behind my back.'

▊ *Filtering out the positive,* for example a focus on wanting validation from the single person who criticised you rather than noticing the many who support you.

▊ *Over-generalising or labelling,* for example: 'I'm useless.'

As well as the ways in which you can challenge them:

▌ *Identify concrete evidence,* for example find evidence for or against the thought in its entirety.

▌ *Categorising,* for example identifying the thought category as one of 'unhelpful thinking'.

▌ *Be the coach,* for example what would I say to a friend who had this thought?

▌ *Look* forward, for example how will I feel about this in 3/6/12 months' time?

▌ *Look for the alternative,* for example is there another way of viewing this situation?

(NHS Scotland, 2018)

Try this exercise.

EXERCISE 8.5

1. Using the table below, identify a negative statement which you may hold after a setback, for example: 'I'm unlovable' (after a break up) or 'I'm useless' after heavy criticism.

2. Categorise the unhelpful thought.

3. Write down statements (and answers) which challenge the thought.[8]

Negative (or unhelpful) thought	Thought category, e.g. 'Over-generalising'	Challenge
I'm useless	Labelling/ over-generalising	▌ What evidence is there to support that I am useless overall? ▌ What evidence goes against it? ▌ What are my successes?

Negative (or unhelpful) thought	Thought category, e.g. 'Over-generalising'	Challenge

[8]This is an adaptation of the commonly used cognitive behavioural approach to challenging negative automatic thoughts as well as the 'empowering thoughts' exercise presented by Ladkowska *et al.* (2018), which challenges you to find evidence against the negative statement that you hold.

Maintaining your well-being

Once you have learned to build emotional resilience – especially in the face of adversity, attending to your well-being while the waters are calm will help you reinforce and maintain that healthy positivity – which, in turn, supports your performance, especially in your interactions.

Unfortunately, as much as you may not want to admit it, when your body is under emotional pressure ,the reaction is physiological.

Try this exercise (although don't hurt yourself).

EXERCISE 8.6

Take an elastic band and pull at it. If you maintain the pressure, one of two things will happen:

1. It will snap.
2. It will not spring back.

That reflects the way in which your own body responds to a constant level of stress. If you do not learn to alleviate the pressure you are under, your body will make you alleviate it through physical problems such as stomach ulcers, high blood pressure or worse.

Mindfulness will help you recognise when you are feeling under pressure and its techniques can help you temper the effects.

Tips to improve your well-being
Avoid becoming overwhelmed

Meditation, once again, is recommended to build up internal resilience – with the very act of deep breathing promoting positive physiological changes in times of stress. As such, when you wish to do so, please go to www.draudreyt.com/meditations and play the 'Meditation for Inner Strength'.

However, if there is limited time to mediate, try the following exercise.

EXERCISE 8.7

1. Hold an object which is meaningful or personal to you in some way.

2. As you focus on the object, breathe deeply and think about why it is so special – perhaps it is because someone special bought it for you. Whatever that reason, focus on it and, when you see the picture of why that object is meaningful,

brighten the colours, the sounds, the sensations – as if you were experiencing it live.

3. When your experience is vivid and vibrant, enjoy the sensation.

4. Then focus back onto the object and remember that you can always relive that pleasant sensation of warmth by looking at the object again.[9]

For a guided meditation version of the exercise, please go to www.draudreyt.com/meditation and listen to the 'Focus Object' track

---

[9] This is an adaptation of the 'focus object' exercise proposed by Timonen *et al.* (2018), utilising the anchoring technique of NLP.

Celebrate your successes

It has been noted in practice that not all clients who subscribe to mindfulness enjoy the 'calm' style of meditation, so taking this 'energizing' approach, while still with the aim of preventing a feeling of being overwhelmed, may be an option.

Try this exercise.

EXERCISE 8.8

'The showreel'

1. Write down a statement that is important and true of you.

2. Repeat that statement to yourself three times.

3. Now focus on your past achievements (as if you are watching your own personal showreel). Watch those 'highlights' play out in your mind.

4. Repeat your statement again.

5. Now focus on your past achievements of the last week. Watch those 'highlights' in the same way as your showreel.

6. Repeat your statement three times.

This exercise is there to motivate you to focus on your achievements, but the part which asks you to focus on the recent past offers a gentle reminder that you need to keep moving forward and continually doing things that you can be proud of. This will re-energise you to continue looking for a new solution or a different pathway through a current troubling situation.

Again, if you would like a guided version of this exercise, please go to www.draudreyt.com/meditations and play the "Personal Showreel" track.

Conduct a 'well-being audit'

A 'safe' workplace is often a resilient and happy workplace

A 'safe' environment – where support and development structures are clear, where executives operate within a friendly network free from harassment or bullying, where responsibility is preferred over blame, is often the best environment. However, although this may be the aim of the leader, it may not be the reality. Carrying out a 'safety audit' – an informal (and anonymous) survey – of your organisation may also give you insights with regards to the level of well-being within your team.

Try this exercise.

EXERCISE 8.9

Ask members of your organisation to rate the following phrases on a scale of 1–10 (where 10 is very true and 1 is not very true):

▎ I feel cared about at work.

▎ I feel safe at work.

▎ Work is fun.

▎ Everyone is treated fairly.

▌ When I succeed or am good at something, it is recognised.

▌ I can be myself at work.

▌ This is a friendly workplace.

▌ I find work interesting.

▌ My workplace takes bullying and harassment seriously.

▌ I know how to get help when I am stuck with work.

▌ My workplace values my opinions.

▌ I know who talk to if I have a problem.

The answers will give you an insight into how your executives are feeling every day and, if there is a problem, potentially open up a dialogue for further investigation and positive action.

Find a moment to be mindful (formally or informally)

While the suggestions within this chapter – and indeed throughout this book so far – have been specifically activity- or exercise-based, it is worth remembering that mindful practice does not always need to be formal.

Of course, it is possible for you to plan time for meditation, safety audits or analysing and challenging your thoughts, but informal moments of being present can be just as conducive to good mental health and well-being (Kissel Wegela, 2010).

Try this exercise.

EXERCISE 8.10

▌ When out walking, listen to birdsong.

▌ When out walking, take a moment to feel the warmth of the sun.

▌ When having a drink, take a moment to appreciate the sensation as it quenches your thirst.

▌ When eating, take a moment to savour the taste – and see if you can recognise the multitude of flavours.

▌ Treat yourself, just because.

▌ Wear something that is uniquely expressive of you (even if it is not obviously displayed).

▌ Have photos of people – or things – that you love around you (many people say, 'It's ok, they are on my phone' – but just a simple quick glance at an object of affection can generate oxytocin, the bonding hormone.)

Recognise and respect your boundaries

There are simple things that you can do to make your working day more pleasant and, when you practice this, your team will learn (and benefit) from your example:

▌ Go to the toilet when you need to.

▌ Stretch your legs by taking a short walk during the day.

▌ Remember to drink water.

▌ State and maintain your office hours (and switch your phone/laptop off at a certain time each night).

▌ Practise saying, 'I'll let you know later' if you cannot yet say 'No' directly.

▌ Practise saying, 'I can only give you X time now' (and stick to it).

▌ Practise the techniques in the earlier part of the chapter to build your emotional resilience, as this will also contribute to greater well-being. (These techniques set boundaries for yourself!)

Remember that setting boundaries not only protects your own emotional strength when you do so internally, for example through challenging unhelpful thoughts, but they make it clear to others when you are available to help them, and sticking to them as much as you can is part of your commitment to valuing yourself.

When you value yourself, you will take care of your well-being – and so will your team.

IN SUMMARY

1. Be aware of, and seek to challenge, the 'myths' which leave a gap in your thinking between expectation and reality.

2. Recognise if you are beginning to engage in 'drowning' or 'blocking' behaviours.

3. Practise reciting positive affirmations to prime your mind to notice the behaviours you want to engage with.

4. Challenge your automatic thought processes by categorising them and using the alternative thinking techniques suggested in this chapter.

5. Check the well-being level within your organisation and team with an informal emotional safety audit.

6. Follow up areas which have been raised within the audit in a supportive, investigative manner to seek resolution.

7. Practise informal moments of mindfulness – the more you practise, the more this will become automatic and the more you will begin to live in (and appreciate) the present.

CHAPTER 8 TOOLKIT

▮ Mindfulness offers leaders personal benefits such as greater mental fortitude, the ability to bounce back after failure, and the strength to keep going even through difficult periods, when there is no one to rely on but yourself.

Key points to remember

1. *Always* reflect on any failure as an opportunity to learn and develop yourself and your team. Ask 'What can I learn?' instead of only 'What went wrong?'

2. *Sometimes* remember to engage in things you enjoy for your personal well-being when you are in a positive mood – do not wait until you are stressed before seeking some form of relaxation.

3. *Try to* recognise your 'blocking' and 'drowning' behaviours as well as identifying what triggered them.

Take action

1. **Reframe**

Next time you catch yourself engaging in 'blocking' (e.g. ignoring something, misusing alcohol) or 'drowning' (e.g. giving up) behaviour, try to note it down and reframe it, using the table below as a guide.

Trigger	Behaviour	What I can do instead

Consider separating the table into 'work-related' and 'personal-related' issues and see if you can identify any patterns in your triggers.

Trigger (W = work-related; P = personal-related)	Behaviour	What I can do instead

If you identify patterns, what can you do to avoid or lessen those triggers?

1.

2.

What I tried

Date	Action

What worked for me

Date	Action

Please use a separate piece of paper if necessary.

Meditation techniques
Guided exercise: focus object

Hold an object that is meaningful or personal to you in some
way.

As you focus on the object, breathe deeply and think about
why it is so special – perhaps it is because someone special
bought it for you. Whatever that reason, focus on it and,
when you see the picture of why that object is meaningful,

brighten the colours, the sounds, the sensations – as if you were experiencing it live.

When your experience is vivid and vibrant, enjoy the sensation.

Then focus back onto the object and remember that you can always relive that pleasant sensation of warmth by looking at the object again.

Meditation for inner strength

Sit or lie down comfortably in a place where you will not be disturbed. Switch off your phone and your computer.

Focus on your breathing. Breathe in through your nose and out through your mouth and, with every breath, allow yourself to become more and more relaxed. This is a guided meditation for inner strength.

As you breathe, picture a beautiful bright candle. It is sparkling and flickering. As you breathe, see the flame move towards and away from you – but it never goes out.

Breathe nice and deeply, watching that flame sparkle and flicker.

Draw in the energy from the flame as you breathe in and feel it as it warms your whole body.

Reach out towards that flame and, as you draw it towards you, it feels warm and strong – surging, energising, powerful.

The energy travels through your nose and down your torso, into your arms and legs and energises you fully. You feel its warmth and you feel its energy. As you breathe out, your breath re-energises the candle for the next time you breathe in.

Breathe in nice and deeply, drawing in the energy and breathe out energising all that surrounds you.

Breathe in through your nose and out through your mouth.

Just as the candle can brighten a room, so too can you be a light in the darkness. Whether that darkness is surrounding you, or someone close to you, your own energy and your own strength can help you be that brightening light.

You have such power within you. You have the ability to brighten a room. You have the strength to energise everything around you.

Breathe in deeply, drawing in the energy from that candle and breathe out, energising all that surrounds you.

When you are in a place of darkness, revisit this candle – this candle that helps you spread light, that reenergises and recharges you, that gives you the strength to shine all around you. This is your candle and your energy. You are capable of so much. You have so much power within you if you allow yourself to shine.

Breathe in deeply, drawing in the energy from that candle and breathe out energising all that surrounds you.

Breathe in and breathe out.
Breathe in and breathe out.

Remember, you can revisit your candle at any time you feel you need to recharge and re-energise ready to shine.

Breathe in and breathe out.

Enjoy that sensation of recharging, re-energising and being ready to shine.

Focus on your breathing until you are ready to open your eyes and come back to the room.

Guided exercise: the showreel

Before you close your eyes, write down a statement that is important and true of you.

Now close your eyes and remember that statement. Take three deep, centring breaths – in through your nose and out through your mouth. As you do, repeat that statement three times to yourself.

Now, as you continue to breathe deeply and calmly, focus on your past achievements (as if you are watching your own personal showreel). Watch those 'highlights' play out in your mind.

Repeat your statement again.

Now focus on your past achievements of the last week. Watch those 'highlights' in the same way as your showreel.

Repeat your statement to yourself three times.

Remind yourself that you have been able to do so much and are capable of so much more.

When you are ready, you can return to your day.

Be aware of your limitations

The opening questions

▮ Have you ever tried to 'bluff' your way out of a difficult situation? Why?

▮ Have you ever said 'I can do that' only to find you couldn't? What did you do then?

▮ What did you learn from either of the two experiences? (And have you ever done it again? If so, why?)

▮ Thinking about your current role, which areas do you dislike or want to improve?

Effective leaders are mindful of their limitations

> *To be aware of limitations is already to be beyond them.*
> Georg Wilhelm Friedrich Hegel

As a leader, you probably always encourage your teams to ask questions and to be aware of what they do not know so that they can find out. But how much time do you take to do this for yourself? Having to perform a number of tasks within a high-pressure environment can sometimes make you feel as if you are always pushed to the edge of your capability. While this can be exhilarating – and you may even thrive on such adrenaline – taking time to pause, think and learn is essential to avoid derailment.

Leadership derailment is the leader who is '. . . thrown off course' or 'unable to move forward' (Furnham, 2013). This might include being demoted or failing to reach a promotion – even failing unexpectedly when it was thought that you would reach a higher position. Derailment can occur when a leader is unable to adapt their skills to organisational changes or demands. It is maintained when the leader refuses to believe that such adaptive behaviour is in their power to manage.

Furnham goes on to explain that even the leaders with positive skill sets have a 'dark side' that can impact the performance of their positive skills:

▍ A leader who prides themselves on integrity may be rigid or consistently impose their views on others.

▍ The leader who is 'innovative' may be unrealistic or have little attention to the demands they place on people, materials or budget.

▍ The customer-focused or even team-focused leader can be overly 'soft' and unable to make difficult decisions that would 'upset someone'.

Try this exercise.

EXERCISE 9.1

List your top three qualities that make you a good leader:

Top three qualities	The dark side
1.	
2.	
3.	

Now list what the 'dark side' (your potential derailment factors) may be.

It is worth doing a mini-audit on your derailment factors because they can change over time. It is very possible that something which may not have caused you any problems a few years ago is suddenly currently troubling. Similarly, you may have worked so hard on some of the factors that you have overcome them or the climate has evolved and your efforts may be better placed elsewhere.

Your team can benefit too

It is not just you who will benefit from this heightened awareness. You will also benefit your team if they are encouraged to identify their potential derailment factors and also if you take them into account when you are considering them for promotion.

Recruiting to a position is the area which, if you do it correctly at the start, saves a number of problems further down the line.

Try this exercise.

EXERCISE 9.2

Keep on track with mindful succession planning

▊ Think about opportunities which might be arising within your organisation.

▊ List the skills needed for the role now and within the future organisational goals, identifying explicitly any areas of change, i.e. will a job grow from leading a small team to a large or remote team?

▊ List who you would consider for promotion and outline the reasons why.

▊ Repeat the 'dark side' audit for their skills – *ideally, also including behaviours which you have observed as well as speculative point.*

- Consider how they may affect performance as the organisation evolves.
- Identify how they might grow and develop, and how you can support and mentor their progress.

Make your decision based on this broader consideration.

As stated in earlier chapters, leadership can be a lonely place, and sometimes both motivation and conviction in your decisions can come only from yourself. This means that leaders may develop a self-belief, which can turn into arrogance if left unchecked (the 'dark side'!) The most effective and healthy leaders are aware of their darker tendencies, work to improve them – and demonstrate this for their teams as well.

How can awareness of your skills help you?

Try this exercise.

EXERCISE 9.3

Thought experiment

Someone has just challenged your values. How do you respond?

- Smash them – show them who's boss!
- Retreat – perhaps they were right.
- Find out more information – something has to be said, but let's clarify what they meant first.

There is value in any of the approaches – in fact, there will be times when you need to respond aggressively and times when you need to draw back. However, if possible, it never hurts to find out more, especially if it can be done quickly.

If you can reply to a challenge in the first instance with an 'escape clause', you may find that someone behaved out of ignorance rather than malice. Through this approach, not only might graciousness gain you an ally as the situation is resolved without cost and without embarrassment, but they may respond provocatively and you have now revealed more of their hand – making them easier to fight.

Of course, there is not always time to take that path, but awareness of your immediate response will highlight your natural skill (and now also make you aware of alternative actions.) Lueke and Gibson (2016) proposed that mindfulness makes us more aware of our implicit biases and immediate behaviour choices. While meditation does not remove an 'automatic association', it helps the person to recognise and manage such a response. While Lueke and Gibson studied prejudice, it is also possible that we may become more aware of other unconscious processes in a similar manner.

Try this exercise.

EXERCISE 9.4

If you have five minutes, download and listen to the short mindful meditation for recognising and breaking habits.

Can you be too aware of limitations?

While awareness of limitations is important for effective leadership and development on a practical level, taking a deeper standpoint – is it possible to be too aware? Ben-Zeev (2010) warns that sometimes it is possible to be overly aware of limitations leading to incongruity and then depression. The three key incongruities are:

1. Human desire is almost infinite and limitless, but human capability is both finite and limited.

2. Undesirable experiences we do not want eventually may occur in our lives (Ben-Zeev cites the example of simply growing old.)

3. Knowledge of what is within our capability to maintain, but that which we do not wish to pursue.

The myth 'Work hard and you will achieve whatever you want' can also negatively impact (and derail!) high-flying executives: '. . . in the messy real world, it is impossible to do everything perfectly at the same time. You cannot pursue all your goals simultaneously or satisfy all your desires at once. And it's an emotional drain to think you can,' (Sinoway, 2010).

The secret to working within human or 'universal' limitations, but breaking through practical ones, is being present and aware of what is under your control.

Try this exercise.

EXERCISE 9.5

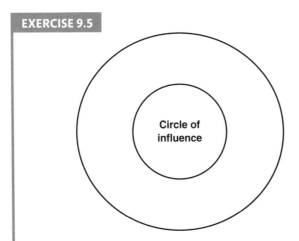

Circle of influence

Write down what you recognise to be your barriers and limitations.

Now 'place' or rewrite them within the circles. In the outside circle, write things over which you have no influence; within the inner circle, write those over which you have.

Pick one of the items in the circle of influence (inner circle) and identify how you can work on it:

Being aware of your limitations makes you focus on what is realistic in both the practical and philosophical sense.

How do I accept I cannot really 'have it all'?

This, for Sinoway (2010), is the hardest thing for most executives and leaders to accept. Not only are there universal limitations but, even within what you can influence, you may need to prioritise and sacrifice. Mindfulness, especially when it comes to explicitly identifying your priorities, helps you to relinquish consciously what you wish to rather than accidentally dropping something that turns out to be important to you. Sinoway identified seven key areas of priority that executives often try to balance and, being able to see which is the most important and which you are devoting the greatest amount of time to, can help you break some bad habits you may have fallen into.

Try this exercise.

EXERCISE 9.6

Look at the following table. For each category, indicate how important it is to you and then indicate the amount of time you are currently devoting to it.

In responding to the first question, explicitly ask yourself: given that I have a finite amount of time and resources, how important is this dimension to me in relation to the others?

Date: _____

Family	Friendship/ community	Spiritual outlook	Physical health	Material possession	Hobbies (non-vocational)	Career prospects

For example:

Family	
Importance level	
Time currently devoted	

Note that, while this exercise is suggested with holistic priorities, it can also be done with leadership tasks, for example:

Team motivation	Improving department	Organisational growth	Team development	Meeting targets	Etc.

Making what is important (and realistically achievable) explicit, as well as identifying the time you are putting into that particular area (and what you may be sacrificing to do so), will help you manage your behaviours and choices to achieve overall fulfilment. While this may still not mean you will ever 'rule the world', you can at least make the corner of the universe which is under your influence more enjoyable. Real change is always healthier, both emotionally and physically, compared with wishful change!

Being aware – or mindful – of your limitations, along with your areas of strength '. . . is an important way to creating intrapersonal integrity, mental and relational health, and being [y]our best selves at work,' (d'Aubermont Thompson, 2017). It is a way in which you can 'pause' life's treadmill and focus on what really matters to you. Attending to your present situation 'warts and all' also prevents you from being blind-sided or derailed by habit or by behaviours which no longer serve you. This temporary moment of reflection enables the actions you take to be effective as they are deliberate and meaningful. As well as this serving you personally, approaching your leadership role holistically offers you greater overall fulfilment and, with that, longevity.

IN SUMMARY

1. Taking a realistic look at your limitations means that you know the areas that you need to focus on or develop in order to stay on track.

2. Sometimes the skills which make you a strong leader can have a 'dark side', which can throw you off course if you are not mindful of it.

3. Remember that you are 'only human' and it is not necessarily always possible to 'have it all'. Therefore, take the time to reflect on your priorities and how much time you are actually investing in each of them . . . especially the ones most important to you.

4. Affording yourself time to reflect enables you to regain control of your life and the direction in which you wish to take it.

CHAPTER 9 TOOLKIT

▮ It is always better to recognise your own potential derailment factors and work on them before they throw you off course.

▮ Being aware of your limitations is a starting point for growth.

Key points to remember

1. *Always* make time to reassess your priorities and the amount of time you are devoting to each of them.

2. *Sometimes* take a moment to think about your response and identify if it is a habitual one.

3. *Try to* consider alternative options to the familiar situations that you face.

Take action

1. **If you catch yourself in an habitual action**

▮ Consider an alternative course of action.

▮ If it might work better – follow it.

▮ Praise yourself for actively doing something different and add that alternative to your repertoire of options.

▌ Reflect on how well that action worked for you and what you could do next time.

2. **Reflect on the exercise in the chapter where you identified a 'dark side' to your top three leadership skills**

Identify ways in which you can recognise and mitigate the effects of the 'dark side'.

	Trigger/'dark side' behaviour	How I can mitigate it
1.		
2.		
3.		
For example	Always taking the moral high ground in a dispute, making me less compassionate	Avoid seeing the issue alone and see the person. Try to vocalise when you recognise the opposing side has made a good point.

Also, you might consider:

▌ encouraging/seeking a 360° appraisal from friends or your team

▌ working with a mentor/coach.

3. **Also, always consider potential derailment factors when picking your team**

Name	Skill	Potential/ observed 'dark side'	Support I can offer

What I tried

Date	Action

What worked for me

Date	Action

Please use a separate piece of paper if necessary.

Meditation techniques

Guided meditation to recognise and break habits

This guided meditation will help free you from the things that are holding you back. Make sure you are sitting or lying comfortably. Switch off your phone and shut down your computer so you can get the full benefit of this time to reflect and recharge.

Breathe deeply and calmly and begin to picture a beautiful scene of sparkling water and a dock. You can hear the waves and smell the fresh air.

Breathe in through your nose and out through your mouth.

Listen to the waves, breathe that fresh air and enjoy the feeling of being so relaxed, so calm, so positive.

You look towards the dock and you see there is something on it and you move towards it.

As you approach the dock, you can see that it is a number of containers. They may be stacked, they may just be lying around.

As you get closer, you can see that they are labelled. They are labelled with all the things that have been holding you back. Look at those labels – perhaps they say fear, self-confidence, body-image, expectation . . . *you* know what those labels are – read them, see them clearly.

Even take a moment to open some of those containers. What images from that barrier do you see? Is it old school reports? Maybe it is old feelings of hurt, envy or disappointment. Maybe it is things that remind you of people who have let you down. Recognise those labels. Recognise that those things in those containers have been holding you back. Recognise also that they do not have to hold you back forever.

Breathe in through your nose and out through your mouth.

You look around the dock again and you notice a raft tied up. Close up those containers and start loading them onto the raft. Rhythmically, easily, lift, walk and load, lift, walk and load . . . it doesn't matter how many there are, the raft can hold all of them. As you load, you realise that you are not tired, in fact, as you continue loading the boxes, you feel stronger and stronger – as if the weight that you have been holding onto is lifting.

Lift, walk, load.

Lift, walk, load.

Continue until all the boxes are loaded.

When they are loaded, look at the boxes on the raft, see the labels, see the things you have been carrying around with you for so long.

Breathe in the fresh air of freedom. In through your nose and out through your mouth. Enjoy that feeling of the weight you have been carrying being lifted.

When you are ready, walk to the raft. Untie the rope which is holding the raft to the dock and left the raft go.

Watch the raft as it begins to sail away, taking all the boxes with it – taking all the things that you have been carrying for so long.

Watch those boxes get smaller and smaller as they float off into the distance.

Those things in the boxes have helped you grow. Those things have helped shape who you are and they will be a part of you, but they do not need to burden you. They have served their purpose and it is ok to let them go. It is ok to free yourself and move forward, knowing you have learned whatever it was you needed to learn from them at the time.

The boxes on the raft get smaller and smaller until they disappear and now you can see just the sparkling water – fresh and clear.

Breathe in that sensation of freedom and letting go.

Whenever you feel you want to load more boxes, there will always be a raft waiting for you. Sometimes it is not the right time to let something go, sometimes you have been holding onto it for so long you have forgotten it is no longer of use to you. Do not allow those boxes – your barriers – to hold you back any longer. You have learned your lessons from them and you are allowed to move on.

When you are ready, turn away from the dock and walk back towards the room that you are in, feeling freer and positive.

Breathe in through your nose and out through your mouth, relaxed knowing that it is ok to let go.

When you are ready, open your eyes, refreshed, unburdened and ready to get on with your day.

3
part

Mindful growth

Inspiration and growth

The opening questions

▌ What part of your role do you value most as a leader?

▌ How many times have you encouraged, supported or helped others grow – this week?

▌ Which leaders inspire you and why?

Inspiring growth through the workplace

> *Life is like a classroom. Only those who are willing to be lifelong learners will move to the head of the class.*
>
> Zig Ziglar, American author, 2013

Jane Hart (2018) opened her learning and development keynote speech 'The Learning Ecosystem' with three warnings:

1. There is no longer a 'job for life'.
2. Artificial intelligence and robotics is changing the nature of many jobs.
3. Knowledge and skills may be going out of date as fast as they can be learned.

How much has changed since you have been reading this book – or even doing your six-minute meditations?

Realistically, while you may not need to worry about your knowledge being surpassed that quickly – at least not yet – the mindful leader is certainly aware that learning habits have changed. Because a person's career (perhaps even your own) may take them through a number of transitions, learners have to be flexible, skills have to be transferrable and learning is now more independent than it has ever been before.

Simply put – you are reading this book and working through the exercises yourself, whereas, say years ago, to introduce 'mindful practice' you might have had a taster workshop and then training on how to apply the concepts. Learning and development is no longer dependent on the old-fashioned classroom.

Furthermore, if you are learning independently, so too can your team, and the options are plentiful and can be encouraged, for example social media, conferences, TED talks, online forums, all alongside the training, which can be arranged by the organisation itself. Your team are also constantly learning from you – whether you or they realise it consciously or not.

There is always a role for helping others learn within leadership. This is derived from the 'Servant Leadership' approach (Greenleaf, 1991). While earlier models of leadership focused on the leader as at the 'top of the hierarchy', the 'servant-leader' helps others develop – and in doing so generates higher performance and fulfilled employees. Maslow (1971) described this as achieving self-transcendence '. . . the very highest and most inclusive or holistic levels of human consciousness, behaving and relating, as ends rather than means, to oneself, to significant others, to human beings in general, to other species, to nature and to the cosmos'. This was the ability to move beyond development for individuals but progress the development of others for the good of society. On a smaller scale, this is the ability to help others grow.

Many leaders see the benefits in nurturing their teams – not least because a team of highly skilled people is better than the leader alone. However, it is not just hard skills being referred to. Even Maslow mentions the 'holistic' nature of self-transcendence and this emphasises, once again, the important role that mindfulness has to play in leadership. Wijebandara (2016) summarised John Quincy Adams (sixth president of the USA): '. . . a leader is one whose actions inspire others to dream more, learn more, do more and become more.' He goes on to state the qualities expected of a leader as identified by his college students: 'Integrity, vision, persuasion, adaptability, generosity' being some of the most important. More importantly, Wijebandara (2016) argues, leadership is long lasting when it is not imposed, but rather, when followers are encouraged to learn and grow to become equals. This is also the essence of Buddhism, the foundation of mindfulness.

Therefore, building on and bringing together the personal and professional work covered in the earlier chapters, this chapter looks at how applied mindful practice with a focus on creating a positive contemporary learning environment can help you develop and grow your team, as well as help you become the best inspirational figure you can be.

How can my self-development inspire my team?

In her book *Mindful Leadership* (2012), Maria Gonzales emphasises the importance of compassion within leadership. The act of helping others is not only of benefit to those being helped, but to those who witness it. She tackles the 'self-care' proviso (one must be emotionally, mentally and physically healthy before helping others) by reminding the reader that compassion is '. . . deep caring without attachment . . . ' and that it is possible to show support without being drawn into the situation yourself.

Furthermore, while your own self-development means you are better able to adapt to a changing world (Reichard and Johnson, 2011), it is also very possible to influence the personal growth of your team through their acknowledgment of what you are doing.

In an even more direct way, in becoming more open and self-reflective, you will have other opportunities to influence others, which previously you might have hidden.

EXERCISE 10.1

Thought experiment

Have you hidden a failure? What was it? What have you learned from it? Maybe there are some exam grades you never talk about. Maybe you're hiding a relationship that didn't work out. However, if you just repress it somewhere, you will never learn the lessons the failure is trying to teach you. Just because you have left an experience on the cutting room floor, learn and inspire others through what you learned from the deleted scene.

Experience of your own ability to come through failure can empower and inspire others as much as success. Hanley (2017) suggests that mindfulness can also help enhance the belief that we have the capacity to meet challenges (even when we have experienced failure in the past). He studied the effect of mindful practice on student beliefs about failure, finding that the higher the self-report on mindful behaviours (such as awareness, openness, managing impulses), the more likely they were to maintain belief in their academic behaviours after failure.

Don't throw the game

How can you let mediocrity win?

Freddie Trumper, *Chess* by Tim Rice,
Benny Andersson, Björn Ulvaeus

Towards the end of the musical *Chess,* the character Freddie Trumper tells his one-time rival Anatoly Sergievsky to play for the win rather than throw the game. The reason was not any hidden political or romantic agenda, but because he loved and valued the game too much to see its play compromised.

Sometimes, for the sake of a hidden agenda, popularity or, even, compassion, you may feel the need to 'throw the game' or deliberately perform badly. In some premeditated occasions, this may be an example of 'Skilled incompetence' (Argryis, 1986) where a leader gifted with emotional intelligence may sabotage their performance to prevent a lack of ability being discovered. For example, if that leader does not know how to address points raised in a memo, they may 'bury it in a drawer' until such time it has been forgotten and, when found out, merely admit to 'forgetting about it' – 'forgetting' (incompetence) being easier to forgive than the lack of ability to deal with the issues.

The act of avoiding an issue to prevent someone else from difficulty is just as disempowering. You are not helping anyone through protecting them, nor yourself. Better to face the areas which need development and take steps to nurture your talents in there.

How can my practice grow and develop my team?

Once you are confident in being a role model for continued personal development, you can structure your organisation to value continuous learning as well. According to Yeganeh and Kolb (2009), mindfulness is one of the best ways to cultivate intentional and thoughtful action within an organisation. With much current organisational development using the Kolb Learning Cycle – capacity to experience, reflect, think and act, Yeganeh and Kolb propose that mindful practices, such as deep breathing or programming your computer to ask you periodically 'Am I being intentional?' (or a similar reflective question) can help prepare the mind to learn as well as encourage more active engagement with the material being pondered. This can help teams get more out of their training. Beyond that, you can cultivate an organisation of independent learners.

EXERCISE 10.2

Mini 'modern learning' audit

▎ What is currently available for my team to learn and develop?

▎ How much of this is available 'on demand'?

▎ How do I encourage my team to pursue independent learning?

▎ How much do *I* engage in independent learning?*

---

*This last question is a little like telling a child that reading is good for them and not being able to tell them what *you* are currently reading. Independent learning is as much the practice of 'do as I do' as well as making the options for it available.

Hart (2018) also said that, with an emphasis on independent learning and growth, there is a need to recruit for 'learnability' rather than the soft skills alone. Sullivan (2015) suggests a number of methods that can be used to assess the ability to learn of interview candidates. These include:

▮ Use a technical question to assess the level of learning and ask for an explanation on the process used to solve the question.

▮ Ask candidates to identify their learning goals and the resources they currently use.

▮ Ask candidates about what they have chosen to study independently.

Once you have included learning ability as part of your selection criteria, make sure you have the resources in place to nurture that skill. This might include:

▮ providing the time to learn

▮ encouraging staff to ask for 'stretch assignments'

▮ requesting feedback yourself

▮ making a point of learning, and perhaps sharing that learning, every week

▮ keeping up to date with developments in your field and making your team do the same – perhaps through asking different people to lead an 'updates' or 'learning and development' section on a weekly briefing.

Promote growth through acknowledging the 'dark side' of highly skilled team members

In the previous chapter, derailment factors were discussed, so this will not be covered at length here. However, it is important to be mindful of your high-fliers – especially those recruited for ability to learn. Those who seem to make multi-tasking look easy, who are always first off the mark in responding to anything required or who are quick to jump at opportunities to learn more, may also be over-thinkers. In itself, wide and critical thinking and broad analysis is a very helpful trait when it comes to self-development, decision making or dealing with arising issues, but it can also have a very negative side. The high-flier can become very consumed with matters beyond their concern and influence if they have little clarity on how to channel their energy efficiently.

If you or members of your team:

▌ dread one-word replies

▌ are always seeking more information

▌ want to get everything right

▌ always need to know 'why'

▌ find it difficult to let things go

(adapted from McKibben, 2018)

. . . then chances are you (or they) are over-thinkers.

The over-thinker is excellent at critical analysis and information gathering – which makes them good at their jobs. Plus, the ability to (over) think is most likely to be praised with comments such as, 'I don't know how you fit it all in' and 'You know so much about everything' because the benefit of over-thinking is knowing quite a lot about a number of things . . . many of which will not be relevant to the problem at hand. What exacerbates this is the very ease at which it is possible to access information and this means that an over-thinker can work themselves into a state of anxiety while gathering more and more information . . . which may or may not be of use. It's a bit like the proverbial hamster on the wheel.

What is important for over-thinkers to do is:

▌ break the cycle of over thinking, when you recognise you are caught in one

▌ learn to focus on what is within your direct influence

▌ appreciate that 'rainy days' will come, sometimes they will pour and you cannot always control that . . . but you can prepare for it.

Mindful practice helps with all of this – and not just through meditations (although any of the meditations accompanying this book may be used at any time).

Try this exercise.

EXERCISE 10.3

1. Use thought stopping to break the cycle of over-thinking when you recognise it

Thought stopping is a cognitive behavioural therapy technique of saying 'Stop' or 'no' out loud (or making another sharp noise) when you recognise that you are getting into a cycle of negative thinking. A word of warning – it may be better to do this in private.

2. Accept that rainy days come – and sometimes they will pour

Try channelling your energy into your physical and mental well-being so that you are fit to face them when they do. Eat well, exercise, see friends, hug a pet – do the things that make you feel good long term.

The inspiring – and tangible – benefits of the 'here and now'

Once your mind stops rushing, it is possible to enjoy the present. Sprinting from one goal to the next without learning from – and taking a moment to enjoy – success is as unhealthy and ineffective for the leader as wallowing in the past, reviewing mistakes and reliving bad experiences without taking action to overcome them. When you focus on the here and now you are '. . . less reactive . . . able to regulate [your] emotions . . . [and can] shift it into how . . . [you] understand and create change.' (Steidle, 2017).

Not only that, but you maximise your engagement with the tasks at hand.

Try this exercise

EXERCISE 10.4

▌ Switch off your phone/leave it in a desk or bag during meetings (so you are not even distracted by a vibration).

▌ Conduct meetings away from your workstation so you are not distracted by your computer.

▌ Negotiate time to speak with your team rather than stopping what you are doing, even for a 'quick question'.

You might even find that your team also do the same.

Such behaviour also has the benefit of signalling to your team, 'I'm here, I care about you. I'm listening and what I am telling you to do is not just based on my own personal opinion but what I'm observing and hearing from you' (Cuddy, 2015). It builds trust, which in turn retains your following.

As a leader, you will always be a role model for someone – and it is better that you are a positive one in deed and in position. Applying mindful practice to your daily life will bring benefits both personally and professionally. Keep going.

IN SUMMARY

1. Leaders retain followers through inspiring and empowering them rather than imposing power over them.

2. Helping your team to grow is part of self-transcendence where you give back to others and in doing so improve your segment of the world.

3. Being able to see a leader's own commitment to self-development sets a positive example to the team.

4. Another means to inspire growth is to create an organisational learning ecosystem which offers multiple opportunities for independent learning.

5. Recruit for learning ability, but also be mindful that positive skills have a potential 'dark side'.

6. Be present in the 'here and now' within your leadership role. It benefits your performance and your relationship with your team.

CHAPTER 10 TOOLKIT

▐ The most effective and inspiring leaders motivate others to '. . . do more and become more!' (John Quincy Adams).

▐ The traits most valued in leaders are the interpersonal ones which encourage teams that they can become equals.

▐ Longevity in leadership is through inspired followers rather than imposition of power.

Key points to remember

1. *Always* remember that in your leadership position you are a role model.

2. *Sometimes* try modelling the self-development behaviour you want, sometimes try teaching it.

3. *Try to* cultivate a reflective, adaptable and empowered learning organisation through recruitment and procedural and training practice.

Take action

1. **Remind yourself to continue to inspire and grow through practising this daily affirmation**

'I'm going to become a better version of myself

'I'm going to start living up to my potential

'I'm going to become the person I was meant to be.'

Try this to remind yourself that as a leader you are always inspiring others – sometimes unconsciously

▮ Look at yourself in the mirror.

▮ List three ways in which you might inspire others (these can be practical, physical, intellectual or in any area).

2. **Then try that exercise with your team**

Tell them that, when they are comfortable in themselves, they will often inspire without realising.

Secret inspirational Santa:

▮ Write all the names of your team and put them in a hat.

▮ Take a name from the hat.

▮ Write/state how that person inspires you.

Things might be revealed that each person did not realise.

3. **Challenge yourself – try to do one of these every day**

▮ Complete one random act of kindness.

▮ Offer at least one genuine and justified expression of congratulations at someone else's success (in your personal or professional life).

▮ Express love or attention in the way that someone you care for likes it – not the way *you* like it (five languages: gifts, quality time, compliments, intimacy, acts of service).

What I tried

Date	Action

What worked for me

Date	Action

Please use a separate piece of paper if necessary.

Maintaining a work–life balance

The opening questions

▌ What do you understand by a 'work–life balance'?

▌ If you maintained that balance, what would it look like?

▌ Where have you over-prioritised in the past?

Defining the 'work–life balance'

> *The challenge of work–life balance is without question one of the most significant struggles faced by modern man.*
>
> (Stephen R. Covey, 2007)

Allen and Paddock (2015) define the work–life balance as the ability to approach all the roles one plays (e.g. parent, sibling, leader, architect . . .) with a high level of attentiveness and care. However, while longer working hours was associated with less balance, spending time with children was associated with more. The use of the word 'however' is deliberate, as you may immediately think, 'No, Allen and Paddock are absolutely right. Of course a work–life balance is related to spending time with family.'

The challenge of the work–life balance, *is accepting that there may be no real 'balance', no real 'equality', but that you will have a preference for one of the two areas and, when that preference is clear, then you can tip the scales in your favour* – and that weighting may need to be adjusted many times a week or even several times a day.

Hill (2016) summarised three key work–life balance fallacies from various TED speakers:

▌ Balance means equal (Stew Friedman): no, it means constant shifting and adjusting of your priorities to find satisfaction.

▌ Balance is attainable (Dan Thurman): no, we are all in a constant state of flux.

▌ You can have it all (Jim Bird): no, you have to navigate between varying priorities and find fulfilment in each daily.

Mindful practice can help you identify your priorities. It reminds you to be ever-present to notice when they change and it enables you to attend to those many roles and choices in your life as fully as you can to get as much out of them as you can. If 'balance' doesn't quite exist, mindfulness will at least help you find fulfilment.

Identify your priorities

Try this exercise.

EXERCISE 11.1

1. Identify three things that are most important to you in your life:

▌

▌

2. Note down what you routinely do in the day.

3. Ask yourself: are those three things getting the most attention? If so, great, keep it up, if not, write down one thing you can do to make a change.

4. Do it.

Once you know what is important to you, you know what will give you the most fulfilment. Note that the word 'happy' is not used. Another common fallacy is that, once a goal is achieved or once you have that precious time to engage in something you enjoy, you will 'be happy' – while this may be a means to happiness, *'happy' is a state not a goal.* A goal is a target which needs to be achieved through work; a state can be achieved, just by looking for it. If you want to be happy, you can choose to be happy right now (look at a photo of something or someone that makes you smile, watch a funny video, hug a pet or just hold your finger horizontally between your teeth and your brain doesn't know the difference between a fake smile and a real one) – why wait?

Your time is limited, channel it well

Try this exercise (adapted from Stephen Covey's four disciplines to attain freedom and productivity).

EXERCISE 11.2

1. Out of your priorities, the most important goal for you to achieve today is:

▮

2. What *'lead measures'* must you focus on to achieve them? For Covey (2007), a 'lead measure' is something where the results are 80 per cent or more under your influence.

▮

▮

▮

3. Reflect at the end of the day – did it happen?

The key to this exercise is not just the taking action, but learning to identify on a daily basis what is under your influence to achieve your goals. Much about managing priorities is managing the time you devote to them and, if you are able to channel your energies effectively, you will also become more time-efficient.

Give full attention to your choices

The swirl process is where many people fail . . . under-swirling so it looks more . . . bovine than marbled, or over-swirling so that it just looks muddy.
Dana Velden, *How to Make a Marble Cake,* 2013

Work–life balance is, perhaps, like that marble cake – you need to swirl to your taste – blended, but not muddy, and each person has their own preference and individual method of swirling. Most bakers would agree, however, that when making a marble cake both flavours are first created separately so that is a good place to start.

Know what you want from your working life. Know what you want from your family life. Then chart your pathway. While it is not possible to 'have it all', it is certainly possible to have as much as you can of both if you are clever (and you can revisit Chapter 9 for a reminder of 'working within limitations').

Try this exercise.

EXERCISE 11.3

Live in the moment (do not sacrifice experience in order to seek the next achievement)

Whatever it is you are doing, try to attend to it fully. For example, try reading this chapter without interruptions from emails, texts or calls or without thinking about anything other than what it is saying to you. Enjoy that purity of focus.

Try that again in your next task.

Similarly, Cope and Whittaker (2012) suggest:

Four minutes of brilliance

For four minutes, fully turn your attention to being 'brilliant' at the task at hand, for example 'I am the best mum/dad in the world', 'I am the best listener in the world' or 'I am the best aerobics class member in the world' – and, for those four minutes, really focus on that as your sole purpose. For Cope and Whittaker, after the first four minutes, it become easier to focus on that specific task and you begin to find more enjoyment within it – even if it was something that initially you were not initially motivated to do (e.g. attend an aerobics class). It also means, for those four minutes, that your focus was absolute and your energy fully channelled. Again – enjoy that feeling and reflect on what you got out of it.

Take a moment to reflect and enjoy your successes

> *Experiences are preceded by mind, led by mind, and produced by mind. If one speaks or acts with an impure mind, suffering follows . . . if one speaks or acts with a pure mind, happiness follows like a shadow that never departs.*
>
> *The Dhammapada*

When your mind is calm, focused and efficient, you are more likely to behave in a manner where success flows more easily. Rather than rush from one achievement to the next, take a moment to enjoy it.

Try this exercise.

EXERCISE 11.4

Practise gratitude

Gratitude is not just the act of saying 'thank you', it is appreciation of the reasons for giving thanks. In mindfulness terms, it is a reminder that others contributed to your success and that you are part of a wider network that you can influence, and that can influence you.

1. The gratitude journal

Get into the habit of writing down three things you are grateful for on a regular basis – daily, weekly, monthly. Make sure that, when you do, you note the reasons for it.

For example:

I am grateful for: _____

Because: _____

_____

_____

2. The letter of gratitude

When Martin Seligman became head of the American Psychological Association in the 1980s, he advocated the progression of the field of Positive Psychology. This field of psychology focused on happiness, resilience and thriving beyond 'normal'. One of his exercises was the 'letter of gratitude':

■ Identify a person who helped you in some way.

■ Write a letter to them explaining why you are grateful.

■ If you can, hand deliver it.

The act of hand delivery might reignite a very positive friendship along with all the benefits that entails.

Even if you do not revisit old friends, pressing the pause button occasionally also gives you time to stop and think about what you are doing, and so make active choices as you continue. This is both empowering and motivating.

Within your organisation you might want to consider:

▎ a gratitude wall where staff can post their thanks

▎ proffering thanks in person rather than sending an email

▎ recognising the people who often might not get thanked, e.g. the janitor, the person who replaces the toilet paper, the post clerk.

Remember that company support, opportunities for development, career progression makes any desire for 'success and recognition' more attainable for you and for your team but that is not the only part of satisfaction. Mindful practice, which helps you make better decisions (Chapter 2) or helps you create and innovate within your role (Chapter 3) and relate well with your team (Chapter 4) are as important to reducing workplace stress – which, in turn, has benefits at home (as the anxiety is not carried over): better sleeping habits, engagement in self-care and looking after your well-being (Chapters 7–9), which see you becoming fresher and more energised, will also have benefits in the workplace. Implementing a mindful approach within the organisation will not only bring these rewards to your team, but also may retain their excellence for longer.

To return to the research by Allen and Paddock (2015) from the start of the chapter, mindfulness specifically helped:

▎ minimisation of distractions – enabling time to be better spent when engaged in something

▎ emotion regulation – reducing the amount of conflict personally and professionally

▌ optimisation of resource allocations – channelling time and energy efficiently and effectively

▌ time perception – generating a feeling that there was more time and less rush.

This not only improved perception of the work–life balance, but also *enriched both* aspects.

It is clear that mindful practice is more than just meditation – in fact, there has not been a single meditation in this chapter! *All* of the techniques and exercises in this book will help you gain more clarity, focus, compassion and direction – all the things which will enhance your day-to-day functioning. Hopefully, you will find yourself less stressed, better able to sleep and good humoured, which will help you approach all the people in your personal and professional life more positively and take action more effectively. Through this, you will increase your work–life fulfilment *and* your enhanced awareness will help you recognise when you are losing your 'balance' and help you to take steps to regain it.

IN SUMMARY

1. Approach maintaining a work–life balance as being able to identify your priorities and devote the amount of focus that is right for you to feel fulfilled.

2. Remember the 'balance' is fluid and you will need to adjust to maintain it as your life and your needs change.

3. You have a finite amount of time and energy – channel it appropriately and efficiently. Try identifying and using your 'lead measures'.

4. Once you have made your choices, give each pursuit your full attention. Try 'four minutes of brilliance'.

5. Press the pause button to reflect on your success, and be grateful for what you have. This is also a good time to make sure you are still working towards your chosen goals.

CHAPTER 11 TOOLKIT

The work–life balance is something that can be achieved when it is understood for what it is – a constantly changing set of priorities through which you feel fulfilled.

▌ When things are good, remember to stay aware in order to make minor adjustments if the 'balance' is tipping too far away from what you desire.

Key Points to Remember

1. *Always* be mindful of your life priorities and use that to direct the actions you choose and decisions you make.

2. *Sometimes* 'press the pause button' to give yourself time to celebrate, reflect and realign, if necessary.

3. *Try to* engage in the mindfulness techniques of meditation, relaxation and gratitude to generate the peace of mind that will support your personal and professional life.

Take action

1. **Try Covey's 'disciplines' exercise for your long-term goals**

▌ Out of your priorities, identify the three most important goals for you to achieve this month/this year

(a)

(b)

(c)

▌ Identify what *'lead measures'* you must focus on to achieve them. (Remember, this is an action where the results are 80 per cent or more under your influence.)

▌

▌

▌

▌ Reflect at the end of the time specified – did it happen?

2. **Identify the signs of an unhealthy work–life balance – for** *you* **and when you recognise them, take the time to reassess your behaviours**

▌

▌

▌

▌

▌

3. **If it helps – schedule 'down time' into your calendar and disconnect during holiday times, evenings and weekends through setting an 'out of office' on your email and voicemail**

4. **If there is a task you find tiring that you cannot avoid, for example a long commute, find a means of making it more pleasurable (with the commute) by downloading podcasts to listen to or reminding yourself that this can be *'you* time'.**

What I tried

Date	Action

What worked for me

Date	Action

Please use a separate piece of paper if necessary.

Epilogue – beyond mindfulness

The opening questions

▍ Which (if any) mindfulness techniques have you implemented in your daily life? (Take a moment to think about how they have helped your performance.)

▍ What (if any) techniques have you suggested to others?

▍ What will you do now to progress your mindfulness practice?

Extending your learning

Becoming a leader is synonymous with becoming yourself. It is precisely that simple, and it is also that difficult.

Warren Gamaliel Bennis, 2014

Using mindfulness to improve your performance is not like learning other skills. The techniques in this book are there to enhance and benefit what you do, and they will still be there whenever you need them. You do not need to keep practising them for fear of 'losing the skill' but, rather, if you enjoy meditation and stop practising, you may feel as if you are missing that time for yourself. Similarly, sometimes, certain techniques may be more helpful than others – and, if a technique is less effective one day, it does not mean that it will not work in future. Mindfulness is another means of investing in yourself.

Everything you learn, everything you adapt, change or flex is a *bonus* to the foundation that is already there. You are assimilating new knowledge and growing even more with it, in the same way as you collaborate with your team or partner with other organisations to bring you to more than before. Not because the path you were on was wrong, but because mindful practice supplements what you already have, allowing you to better recognise, appreciate and utilise it.

In particular, the practice of mindfulness is of great support to leaders already practised in emotional agility. For those who are gifted at supporting, motivating and getting the best out of others, mindfulness enables you the time to focus on yourself. This helps you recharge as well as protect yourself against the many demands of performing emotional labour. As stated in the previous chapter, mindfulness is not just about better performance, it is about self-protection (which, in turn, aids performance and longevity).

Mindfulness, as stated at the very beginning of this book, promotes openness and implicit awareness of yourself and of others. With it, it generates kindness and compassion – traits important to the modern leader, especially one who is moving towards self-transcendence (Maslow, 1971). While you may note, as Wuthnow (1995) did, that the most prominent show of true kindness often is found within the natural instinct of the child but *they learn to suppress it as they grow older – for fear of seeming weak,* and there may be grounds for fearing kindness as a source of creating weak-ness. However, kindness and compassion bring extraordinary benefits to the workplace, as you will have recognised, but where it has a 'dark side', some channelling may be required and, perhaps, support for the labourer whose compassion may overwhelm them (Riley, 2010).

There will be ideas in this book that inspire you, activities which help you and directions revealed that may suit your needs – and there will be things that will not be as much use. This doesn't matter. Part of mindful (and indeed *efficient*) practice is knowing actively what works for you and what doesn't. Practising mindfulness is just one of many techniques available to you to help you navigate your course both personally and professionally in order to choose the life that you want.

Where do I go from here?

If the exercises in this book benefit you, repeat them. Try the different meditations included and use the internet or alternative resources for more – often it is more about finding a 'voice' and a style which you enjoy rather than specific topics for meditations.

Read more about mindfulness, download apps, even consider teaching it – but a word of caution, at the time of writing, as with much of the more holistic approaches to psychology, there is little regulation on mindfulness training programmes for teachers.

There may even be alternatives to mindfulness which you prefer. The Danish practice of *Hygge* (pronounces 'hooga') from a Norwegian meaning 'well-being' focuses on building a lifestyle which brings about '. . . a warm atmosphere. It is enjoying the good things in life with good people,' (Visit Denmark, 2018). However, it is well to note that the Danish lifestyle is more set up for this with better civic support, a cleaner environment, social support (OECD, 2017). Although the working hours can average around 49 hours per week, the Danes themselves prioritise their home lives (Gray, 2017).

Alternatively, perhaps you wish to take up yoga or learn more about Buddhism – again, the internet is a good starting point to find local classes where you will also get the community benefits of meeting likeminded people and sharing your experiences.

Being more fulfilled within your life and your performance as a leader are inter-linked with elements that can be exclusive. While choosing not to practise mindfulness may not affect your performance short term because of all the skills and experience you have built up, you may miss out on the benefits that it entails or, perhaps, not be strong enough to come through the next setback.

What you choose now is up to you – remember to always make it an *active* choice.

IN SUMMARY

1. Mindful practice techniques are there to enhance your current performance.

2. Always use what works for you – if something doesn't work at one point in time, leave it and consider coming back to it at a later point.

3. While compassion is a good thing for the leader, make sure it is channelled and supported to avoid fatigue or burnout.

4. You can enhance your mindfulness practice through wider reading or even experimenting with the alternatives such as yoga, *Hygge* or Buddhism, but the exercises in this book will always be there, should you need them.

CHAPTER 12 TOOLKIT

▌ Anything that helps you to be more aware of your being, enables you to take relaxed yet empowered action driven by choice rather than habit and supports you in your compassion towards others may be considered mindful practice.

▌ If it works for you – and makes you feel better – use it, if not, it's ok to find something else (healthy) that does.

Key points to remember

1. *Always* incorporate mindfulness into your day, whether it is just taking a moment to pause and reflect or one of the longer techniques.

2. *Sometimes* read more about the areas of mindfulness that interest you and adapt and develop your practices.

3. *Try to* show compassion to yourself, whether this is in using kind language or practising self-care – being mindful is just an *enhancement* to daily practice.

---

[10] Seet Chee Kim is the author's grandfather. He taught Practical Buddhism in Youth Circles, Dharma Schools, and Buddhist Societies in Malacca, Malaysia.

Take action

1. **Reflect on the following 10 'practical Buddhism' teachings adapted from Seet Chee Kim's[10] teachings of Buddhism within everyday life.**

Think about how their meaning can help your own conduct for:

Learning without thought is labour lost.

(Seet, 1961)

i. Just as the light of a single candle has the power to dispel darkness in a room, so also the light developed in one person can help dispel the darkness in several others. Use your learning to light the way.

ii. By controlling our actions we gain mastery of the moment which will bring us nearer to our real self. Remember that you are always in charge of your choices and actions.

iii. A person evolving more gradually than you will have ideas and ideals which you have outgrown. Assist them by example and understanding and not by intolerance.

iv. You do not have to prove to others that you consider the path you have chosen is the right one – you need only believe for yourself that it is the right one for you, and always bear in mind that it is not necessarily so for others. Avoid offering unsolicited advice if you can!

v. Right understanding is of very little value unless it is accompanied by right conduct. The two must go hand in hand. If you believe in it – apply it!

vi. 'Manners maketh a man' – when you become a leader, do not look altogether to wisdom, ability or character, but partly also to manners, to those who can get on well with others. Recruit for traits and values that are meaningful in the context of work being social.

vii. The true method of education is to question all things. Remember to always think critically – even of your own findings.

viii. Character and steadiness will do more for a man than cleverness. It is more important to do right than to know it.

ix. Never do anything which will give you cause to be ashamed. There is one good opinion which is of the greatest importance to you – your own.

x. Be honest and truthful. It is well to be ashamed of yourself if you are in the wrong, but never be ashamed to own it. Have the course to be true and have the conviction to be what you are.

2. **Write down the names of local groups, websites or books that will enhance your mindful practice further:**

_____

_____

_____

_____

_____

_____

_____

_____

_____

_____

_____

What I tried

Date	Action

What worked for me

Date	Action

Please use a separate piece of paper if necessary.

References

Introduction

Barnett, E. (2015) 'Mindfulness: The saddest trend of 2015', *The Telegraph,* http://www.telegraph.co.uk/women/womens-life/11331034/Mindfulness-the-saddest-trend-of-2015.html. Accessed 25 July 2017.

Bodhi, B. (2013) *What does mindfulness really mean? A canonical perspective* cited in Williams, M.G. and Kabat-Zinn, J.(2013) *Mindfulness: Diverse Perspectives on Its Meaning, Origins and Applications,* Routledge.

Confino, J. (2014) 'Google's head of mindfulness: "goodness is good for business"', *The Guardian,* http://www.theguardian.com/sustainable-business/google-meditation-mindfulness-technology. Accessed 15 January 2018.

Gelles, D. (2012) 'The mind business', *Financial Times* http://www.ft.com/cms/s/2/d9cb7940-ebea-11e1-985a-00144feab49a.html#axzz2ApW2UUXh. Accessed 15 January 2018.

Gelles, D. (2015) 'At Aetna, a C.E.O.'s Management by Mantra', *The New York Times,* http://www.nytimes.com/2015/03/01/business/at-aetna-a-ceos-management-by-mantra.html?_r=0. Accessed 15 January 2018.

Intel Newsroom (2013) *'Better Engineering through Meditation?',* https://newsroom.intel.com/editorials/better-engineering-through-meditation-mindfulness/. Accessed 4 July 2018.

Note to Self Podcast (2018) 'Dan Harris Knows All Your Excuses for Not Meditating' https://www.wnyc.org/story/dan-harris-meditation-skeptics. Accessed 12 January 2018.

Whippman, R. (2016) *America the Anxious: How Our Pursuit of Happiness Is Creating a Nation of Nervous Wrecks,* St Martin's Press.

Williams, R. (2016) *How Mindful Leaders Can Transform Organisations,* www.psychologytoday.com. Accessed 26 December 2017.

Chapter 1

Burchard, B. (2017) *High Performance Habits: How Extraordinary People Become That Way,* Hay House Inc.

Davidson, R.J. and Lutz, A. (2008), 'Buddha's Brain: Neuroplasticity and Meditation', *IEEE Signal Process Magazine,*1 January; 25 (1):174–76.

Fort Garry Women's Resource Centre, California (2018), 'Self-care for women: fact sheet', http://www.fgwrc.ca/uploads/ck/files/Resources/Factsheets/FactSheetSelfCare.pdf. Accessed 15 January 2018.

Goleman, D. (2017) 'Here's What Mindfulness Is (and Isn't) Good for', *Harvard Business Review,* https://hbr.org/2017/09/heres-what-mindfulness-is-and-isnt-good-for. Accessed 9 October 2017.

Ling, N.E. and Chin, G.H. (2012) 'Mindfulness and Leadership', http://www.vizenllc.com/wp-content/uploads/2015/07/MindfulnessAndLeadership.pdf. Accessed 9 October 2017.

MacKinnon, M. (2016) 'The Science of Slow Deep Breathing', *Psychology Today,* https://www.psychologytoday.com/blog/neuraptitude/201602/the-science-slow-deep-breathing. Accessed 5 January 2018.

MAHLE Powertrain (2017) Open Lecture, 17 July 2017.

Maslow, A. H. (1970) *Religions, Values, and Peak Experiences.* New York: Penguin (Original work published 1964).

Michel, A., Borsch, C. and Rexroth, M. (2014) 'Mindfulness as a cognitive-emotional segmentation strategy: An intervention promoting work–life balance', *Occupational and Organisational Psychology,* Volume 87, Issue 4, 733–54.

Mindfulnet.org (2017) Home Page http://mindfulnet.org/. Accessed 5 September 2017.

Mudd, P.A. (2015) *Uncovering Mindfulness: In Search of a Life More Meaningful,* Kindle Edition, Amazon, Bookboon.com.

Pidgeon, A.M. and Keye, M.D. (2014) 'Relationship between Resilience, Mindfulness, and Psychological Well-being in University Students', *International Journal of Liberal Arts and Social Science,* 2(5), 27–32.

Shanafelt, T.D., Boone, S., and Tan, L. (2012) 'Burnout and satisfaction within work–life balance in US physicians relative to the general US population', Arch Intern Med. 172(18):1377–85.

Su, A.J. (2017) '6 Ways to Weave Self-Care into your Work Day', *Harvard Business Review,* https://hbr.org/2017/06/6-ways-to-weave-self-care-into-your-workday. Accessed 12 December 2017.

Trisgolio, A. (2017) , 'Mindfulness and Leadership', vizenllc .com, http://vizenllc.com/research/mindfulness/Trisoglio_Mindful_Leadership_Mobius.pdf. Accessed 9 October 2017.

Williams, R. (2016) *How Mindful Leaders Can Transform Organisations,* www.psychologytoday.com. Accessed 26 December 2017.

Chapter 2

Aronson, E. (2017) 'Not By Chance Alone', The Psychology Podcast, November. Accessed 3 January 2018.

Carmichael, A. (2017) 'The Drunken Man', lecture notes, PMI Conference, July, Athens.

Chang, L. (2012) '5 Steps of Effective & Mindful Problem Solving', Mindfulness Muse, https://www.mindfulnessmuse.

com/cognitive-behavioral-therapy/5-steps-of-effective-mindful-problem-solving. Accessed 16 January 2018.

Hafenbrack, A.C., Kinias, Z. and Barsade, S.G. (2013) 'Debiasing the Mind Through Meditation: Mindfulness and the Sunk-Cost Bias' SAGE Journals, http://journals.sagepub.com/doi/abs/10.1177/0956797613503853. Accessed 16 January 2018.

Haidt, J. (2006) *The Happiness Hypothesis,* Arrow.

Insead Knowledge (2014) 'How Mindfulness Improves Decision-Making', Forbes, https://www.forbes.com/sites/insead/2014/08/05/how-mindfulness-improves-decision-making/#76c8f47d728b. Accessed 7 January 2018.

Jazaieri, H. (2014) 'Can Mindfulness Improve Decision Making?' https://www.mindful.org/can-mindfulness-improve-decision-making/. Accessed 16 January 2018.

Ostafin *et al.* (2012) cited in Jazaieri, H. (2014) 'Can Mindfulness Improve Decision Making?' https://www.mindful.org/can-mindfulness-improve-decision-making/. Accessed 16 January 2018.

Papert, S. (1997) In Interview, SFGATE, http://www.sfgate.com/news/article/SUNDAY-INTERVIEW-Seymour-Papert-Computers-In-2856685.php. Accessed 2 February 2018.

Powell, C. (2011) '10 Lessons in Leadership', http://www.au.af.mil/au/afri/aspj/apjinternational/apj-s/2011/2011-4/2011_4_02_powell_s_eng.pdf. Accessed 4 July 2018.

Reb, J., Narayanan, J. and Chaturvedi, S. (2014) 'Leading Mindfully: Two Studies of the Influence of Supervisor Trait Mindfulness on Employee Well-being and Performance', Singapore Management University, https://ink.library.smu.edu.sg/cgi/viewcontent.cgi?article=4319&context=lkcsb_research. Accessed 16 January 2018.

Soonevelt, J. (2017) 'Storytelling to assist decision making', lecture notes, PMI Conference, July, Athens.

Whitbred, S. and Greene, N. (2017) 'Byron's Babbles', blog, https://byronernest.blog/2017/04/04/decision-making-vs-problem-solving-and-why-the-difference-matters/. Accessed 16 January 2018.

Chapter 3

Barak, S. (2016) 'Faces of Innovation: A Personal Perspective on Mindfulness in our Workplace' http://www.ntti3.com/faces-innovation-workplace-mindfulness/. Accessed 31 January 2018.

Beardsley, A .(2016) NLP Practitioner Course, Lecture Notes, Excellence Assured, https://excellenceassured.com/. (Course taken, July 2016).

Goh, C. (2016) 'How to Apply Mindfulness to the Creative Process', https://www.mindful.org/apply-mindfulness-creative-process/. Accessed 31 January 2018.

Latino, B. (2013) 'Improving Reliability with Root Cause Analysis' https://www.psqh.com/analysis/improving-reliability-with-root-cause-analysis/. Accessed 7 January 2018.

Marshall, D. (2013) 'There's a Critical Difference Between Creativity and Innovation', http://www.businessinsider.com/difference-between-creativity-and-innovation-2013-4?IR=T. Accessed 31 January 2018.

Pfannkuch, K. (2015) 'The Psychological Reasons People Don't Share Their Ideas', Kapost Blog, https://marketeer.kapost.com/why-people-dont-share-ideas/. Accessed 31 January 2018.

Picasso, P. (2013) cited in Penn State Blog, 'Every child is an artist. The problem is how to remain an artist once he grows up', Can I Quote You on That? http://sites.psu.edu/frupertpassion/2013/10/30/every-child-is-an-artist-the-problem-is-how-to-remain-an-artist-once-he-grows-up-pablo-picasso/. Accessed 31 July 2018.

Radjou, N., Prabhu, J., Ahuja, S. and Roberts, K. (2012) *Jugaad Innovation: Think Frugal, Be Flexible, Generate Breakthrough,* John Wiley and Sons.

Schiermeyer, E. cited in Goguen-Hughes, L (2011) 'Mindfulness and Innovation', https://www.mindful.org/mindfulness-and-innovation/. Accessed 6 January 2018.

Schootstra, E., Deichmann, D. and Dolgova, E. (2017) cited in Muir, M. (2017) 'How 10 Minutes of Mindfulness can make Employees more Creative' https://scotlandb2b.co.uk/2018/01/07/how-10-minutes-of-mindfulness-can-make-employees-more-creative/. Accessed 31 January 2018.

Schultz, R. (2014) '6 steps to boost innovation through mindfulness', GreenBiz, https://www.greenbiz.com/blog/2014/04/14/six-steps-truly-open-collaboration-through-mindfulness. Accessed 14 January 2018.

Shallard, P. (2017) 'Wealth, Freedom, Sanity', The Shrink for Entrepreneurs, http://www.petershallard.com/. Accessed 31 January 2018.

Timms, P. (2018) Keynote Speech, Learning and Development Conference, Athens, 30 January. Attended 30 January 2018.

Tournier, I. and Ferring, D. (2017) 'How the Mindfulness Concept Could Benefit the Caregiving of Older Adults', *Innovation in Aging,* (1)(1) 164–165, https://doi.org/10.1093/geroni/igx004.642. Accessed 15 January 2018.

Weick, K.E. and Sutcliffe, K.M. (2007) *Managing the Unexpected,* John Wiley and Sons.

Wiseman, R. (2004) *Did You Spot the Gorilla? How to Recognise the Hidden Opportunities in Your Life.* Arrow.

Music

'Ladies and Gentlemen We are Floating in Space', 1997, Spiritualised from the album *We Are Floating in Space.*

Pachelbel's Canon in D, 1680, Johann Pachelbel.

'We Dance On', 2010, N-Dubz ft. Bodyrox from the album *Love Live Life.*

Chapter 4

Berkrot, B. (2016) 'Biden announces US project to promote cancer data, Reuters, https://www.reuters.com/article/us-health-cancer-genome-idUSKCN0YS1UN. Accessed 4 July 2018.

Bunting, M. (2016) 'How mindfulness can prevent your team from falling apart', *Inside HR,* https://www.insidehr.com.au/how-mindfulness-can-prevent-your-team-from-falling-apart/. Accessed 4 July 2018.

Excellence Assured (2017) NLP training course, lecture notes from the NLP Practitioner Training Course. Course completed June 2017.

Gordon, R., Milano, B., Chotaliya, C. and Carr, H.L. (2018) *The Collaboration Cycle,* Mindfulness in Leadership Programme, Brunel University with CLICK Training, January.

Greenberg, M. (2016) 'Can Mindfulness Make Your Relationship Happier?' *Psychology Today,* https://www.psychologytoday.com/blog/the-mindful-self-express/201606/can-mindfulness-make-your-relationship-happier. Accessed 6 February 2018.

King, R. (1992) Cell phone recording from the Los Angeles Riots, 1 May, https://www.youtube.com/watch?v=1sONfxPCTU0. Accessed 6 February 2018.

Lencioni, P. (2002) *The Five Dysfunctions of a Team,* Josey-Bass.

Mindfulness Works (2017), About Our Workplace Courses, MindfulnessWorks.com, https://mindfulnessworks.com/aboutourworkplacecourses.php. Accessed 28 August 2018.
Ohno, T (1988) *Toyota Production System – beyond large-scale production,* Productivity Press.

Panes, A. (2014) *Why Swarm Organisations are the Future,* Capgemini.com, https://www.capgemini.com/2014/11/why-swarm-organisations-are-the-future/. Accessed 6 February 2018.

Takeuchi, H. and Nonaka, I. (1986) 'The new new product development game', *Harvard Business Review,* January–February.

Timms, P. (2018) Learning & Development Conference, Athens, January.

Chapter 5

David, S. (2016) *Emotional Agility: Get Unstuck, Embrace Change and Thrive in Work and Life,* Penguin.

Excellence Assured (2017) NLP training course, lecture notes from the NLP Practitioner Training Course (Course completed June 2017).

Freud, A. (1937) *The Ego and the Mechanisms of Defence,* London: Hogarth Press and Institute of Psycho-Analysis. (Revised edition: 1966 USA, 1968 UK.)

Green, K.R. (2013) 'The Social Media Effect: Are You Really Who You Portray Online?', https://www.huffingtonpost.com/r-kay-green/the-social-media-effect-a_b_3721029.html. Accessed 4 March 2018.

Hochschild, A.R. (1983) *The Managed Heart,* Berkeley University of California Press.

NLP World (2018) NLP Training – META Model https://www.nlpworld.co.uk/nlp-training-meta-model/. Accessed 4 March 2018.

Yacobi, B.G. (2012) 'The Limits of Authenticity', *Philosophy Now,* https://philosophynow.org/issues/92/The_Limits_of_Authenticity. Accessed 4 July 2018.

Chapter 6

Becker, M.W., Alzahabi, R. and Hopwood, C.J. (2012) 'Media Multitasking is Associated with Symptoms of Depression and Social Anxiety', *Cyberpsychology, Behaviour and Social Networking,* Vol. 16(2).

Dottie, C. (2017) '6 reasons leaders need to raise their social media game, *Silicone Republic* https://www.siliconrepublic.com/advice/leaders-social-media-tips-hays. Accessed 27 March 2018.

Kanter, R.M. (2005) 'How Leaders Gain (and Lose) Confidence', *Leader to Leader,* 35 (21–27).

Karpman, B. (1967, 2007) The New Drama Triangles USATAA/ITAA, Conference lecture, 11 August 2007, free download worksheet for the DVD, https://karpmandramatriangle.com/pdf/thenewdramatriangles.pdf. Accessed 27 March 2018.

Levin, M. (2016) 'How to Avoid the Three Most Dangerous Roles in Leadership (and Life)', www.inc.com https://www.inc.com/marissa-levin/the-three-most-dangerous-roles-in-life-and-leadership-and-how-to-avoid-them.html. Accessed 4 July 2018.

Meshanko, P. (2013) *The Respect Effect: Using the Science of Neuroleadership to Inspire a More Loyal and Productive Workplace,* McGraw-Hill Education.

Riley, P. (2010) *Attachment theory and the student-teacher relationship,* London: Routledge.

Shakespeare, W. (1602) *Hamlet, Prince of Denmark,* Full text: http://shakespeare.mit.edu/hamlet/full.html. Accessed 28 March 2018.

Shakespeare, W. (1603) *Measure for Measure,* Full text: http://shakespeare.mit.edu/measure/full.html. Accessed 28 March 2018.

Smith, S.A. (2014) 'Mindfulness-based stress reduction: an intervention to enhance the effectiveness of nurses coping with work-related stress', *International Journal of Nursing Knowledge*, June 25(2):119–30.

Chapter 7

Altshul, S. (2012) 'The Healing Power of Pine', Health.com, http://www.health.com/health/article/0,,20428734,00.html. Accessed 28 March 2018.

Lamott, A. (2018) '77 Self-care quotes to remind you to take care of yourself', https://www.developgoodhabits.com/self-care-quotes/. Accessed 23 February 2018.

Lisansky Beck, D. (2016) 'Mindfulness: 10 Lessons in Self-Care for Social Workers', *The Social Worker,* http://www .socialworker.com/feature-articles/practice/mindfulness-10-lessons-in-self-care-for-social-workers/. Accessed 4 July 2018.

Markway, B. (2015) 'Your Ultimate Self-Care Assessment (with resources!)', *Psychology Today,* https://www. psychologytoday.com/blog/living-the-questions/201504/ your-ultimate-self-care-assessment-resources. Accessed 23 February 2018.

Moore, D. (2015) cited in Tang, A. (2018) 'Do You Suffer From Seasonal Affective Disorder?', *The Squeeze Magazine,* https://press-london.com/blogs/squeeze/do-you-suffer-from-seasonal-affective-disorder. Accessed 28 March 2018.

Rudgard, O. (2017) Mindfulness can lead to selfishness, warns psychiatry expert, *The Telegraph,* https://www.telegraph. co.uk/news/2017/12/28/mindfulness-can-lead-selfishness-warns-psychiatry-expert/. Accessed 28 March 2018.

Smith, C. (2014), 'Overcoming Low Self-Esteem with Mindfulness', *Psychology Today,* https://www.psychology today.com/blog/shift/201411/overcoming-low-self-esteem-mindfulness. Accessed 23 February 2018.

Tang, A. (2015), *Love's Labours Redressed – Reframing Emotional Labour,* Lap Lambert Academic Publishing.

Chapter 8

Baucells M. and Sarin, R. (2011) *Engineering Happiness,* University of California Press.

Billings, J. (circa 1885) cited by Brainyquote.Com https://www.brainyquote.com/authors/josh_billings. Accessed 4 July 2018.

Burch, V. (2008) *Living Well with Pain and Illness – The Mindful Way to Free Yourself from Suffering,* Piatkus.

Burkeman, O. (2013) 'This column will change your life: The truth about happiness', *The Guardian,* https://www.theguardian.com/lifeandstyle/2013/oct/12/happiness-reality-expectations-oliver-burkeman. Accessed 16 February 2018.

Cambridge Online Dictionary (2018), https://dictionary.cambridge.org/dictionary/english/well-being. Accessed 5 March 2018.

Clough, P. and Strycharczyk, D. (2012) *Developing Mental Toughness: Improving Performance, Wellbeing and Positive Behaviour in Others,* Kogan Page Publishers.

HSE.Gov.UK (2016) *Work-related Stress, Depression or Anxiety Statistics in Great Britain 2017,* http://www.hse.gov.uk/statistics/causdis/stress/stress.pdf. Accessed 5 March 2018.

Kissel Wegela, K. (2010) 'Practicing Mindfulness Without Meditating: How to cultivate mindfulness without meditating', The Courage to be Present, *Psychology Today* https://www.psychologytoday.com/blog/the-courage-be-present/201002/practicing-mindfulness-without-meditating. Accessed 18 February 2018.

Ladkowska, E., Cornforth, J.L., Kajahn, A.K. and Ashton, H. (2018) 'Empowering Thoughts', Mindfulness in Leadership Programme, Brunel University with CLICK Training, January 2018.

Mindful.org (2016) Mindful.org. Accessed 23 February 2018.

NHS Scotland (2018), 'Challenging unhelpful thoughts' http://www.moodjuice.scot.nhs.uk/challengingthoughts.asp. Accessed 17 February 2018.

Timms, P. (2018) Presentation during the Learning and Development Conference, Athens, January 2018.

Timonen, E.A., Ismaelis, A., Hussain, M., Papayiannis, K. and Farah, H. (2018) 'Focus Object', Mindfulness in Leadership Programme, Brunel University with CLICK Training, January 2018.

Wasylyshyn, K.M. and Masterpasqua, F. (2018) 'Developing self-compassion in leadership development coaching: a practice model and case study analysis', *International Coaching Psychology Review,* Vol. 13 (1) 21–34.

White, L. (2015) 'The Most Acceptable Reasons to Take a Sick Day Revealed', *The Independent* http://www.independent.co.uk/life-style/health-and-families/health-news/the-most-acceptable-reasons-to-take-a-sick-day-revealed-a6725831.html. Accessed 5 March 2018.

Wiseman, R. (2003) *The Luck Factor,* Arrow Books.

Chapter 9

Ben-Zeev, A. (2010) 'Darling, Are You Aware of your Limitations?', *Psychology Today,* https://www.psychologytoday.com/us/blog/in-the-name-love/201003/darling-are-you-aware-your-limitations. Accessed 3 April 2018.

d'Aubermont Thompson, N. (2017) 'Mindful of Myself: A Brand New Me?', *Huffington Post,* https://www.huffingtonpost.com/natalie-daubermont-thompson/mindful-of-myself-a-brand-new-me-_b_9044772.html. Accessed 3 April 2018.

Furnham, A. (2013) 'The Dark Side of Leadership Management Derailment', EAWOP conference talk: http://www.eawop.org/ckeditor_assets/attachments/416/worklab_2013_adrianfurnham_talk2.pdf?1384979822. Accessed 3 April 2018.

Hegel, G.W.F. cited in in Davis, W.A .(1989) *Inwardness and Existence Subjectivity in/and Hegel, Heidegger, Marx, and Freud,* University of Wisconsin Press.

Lueke, A. and Gibson, B. (2016) 'Brief Mindfulness Mediation Reduces Discrimination', Psychology of Consciousness: Theory, Research, and Practice, 3(1).

Sinoway, E.C. (2010) 'No, You Can't Have it All', *Harvard Business Review* https://hbr.org/2012/10/no-you-cant-have-it-all. Accessed 3 April 2018.

Chapter 10

Argryis, C. (1986) 'Skilled Incompetence', *Harvard Business Review,* https://hbr.org/1986/09/skilled-incompetence. Accessed 11 April 2018.

Cuddy, A. (2015) *Presence, Bringing your Boldest Self to your Biggest Challenges,* Little Brown and Company.

Gonzales, M. (2012) *Mindful Leadership: The 9 Ways to Self-Awareness, Transforming Yourself, and Inspiring Others,* John Wiley & Sons.

Greenleaf, R. (1991) *The Servant as Leader* (Rev. ed.), Indianapolis, IN: Robert K. Greenleaf Center.

Hanley, A.W. (2017) 'Clarity of Mind: Structural Equation Modeling of Associations between Dispositional Mindfulness, Self-concept Clarity and Psychological Well-being', *Personality and Individual Differences,* Volume 106, 334–9.

Hart, J. (2018) Keynote Speech 'The Learning Ecosystem', Learning and Development Conference, Maroussi Plaza & Conference Centre, Athens, 30 January 2018.

Maslow, A.H. (1971) *The Farther Reaches of Human Nature,* New York.

McKibben, S. (2018) '15 Signs You're An Over-Thinker Even If You Don't Feel You Are', Lifehack.org https://www.lifehack.org/287116/15-signs-youre-over-thinker-even-you-dont-feel-you-are. Accessed 11 April 2018.

Reichard, R.J. and Johnson, S.K. (2011) 'Leader self-development as organizational strategy', *The Leadership Quarterly,* Volume 22, Issue 1, Feb, 33-42.

Rice R, Andersson, B. and Ulvaeus, B. (1986) *Chess: The Musical,* Samuel French Ltd.

Steidle, G.K. (2017) *Leading from Within: Conscious Social Change and Mindfulness for Social Innovation,* MIT Press.

Sullivan, J. (2015) 'Want Top-performing hires? Learning Ability May Be The No 1 Predictor', www.ere.net https://www.ere.net/want-top-performing-hires-learning-ability-may-be-the-no-1-predictor/. Accessed 9 April 2018.

Wijebandara, C. (2016) 'The Buddha's concept of leadership', *The Nation,* http://www.nationmultimedia.com/opinion/The-Buddhas-concept-of-leadership-30286428.html. Accessed 11 April 2018.

Yeganeh, B. and Kolb, D. (2009) 'Mindfulness and Experiential Learning', *OD Practitioner,* http://www.move-up-consulting.net/fileadmin/user_upload/Readings/Mindfulness_and_Experiential_Learning_.pdf. Accessed 11 April 2018.

Ziglar, Z. quoted in Ziglar, Z. and Reighard, D. (2013) *The One Year Daily Insights with Zig Ziglar,* Tyndale House Publishers Inc.

Chapter 11

Allen, T.D. and Paddock, E.L. (2015) 'How being mindful impacts individuals' work-family balance, conflict, and enrichment: A review of existing evidence, mechanisms and future directions', *Mindfulness in Organizations,* Cambridge.

Cope, A. and Whittaker, A. (2012) *The Art of Being Brilliant: Transform your life by doing what works for you,* Capstone 1 Edition.

Covey, S.R. (2007) 'Work–Life Balance: A Different Cut', Forbes.com, https://www.forbes.com/2007/03/19/covey-work-life-lead-careers-worklife07-cz_sc_0319covey.html#54b1e5ee754. Accessed 4 July 2018.

Hill, E. (2016) 'There's No Such Thing as "Work–Life Balance"' *Huffington Post,* https://www.huffingtonpost.com/emily-hill/worklife-balance-is-a-big_b_13272112.html. Accessed 13 April 2018.

The Dhammapada, Chapter 1, verses 1 and 2. Translation by Sangharakshita, available for free download at www .sangharakshita.org. Accessed 13 April 2018.

Velden, D. (2013) 'How to Make a Chocolate & Vanilla Swirled Marble Cake', @Kitchn, https://www.thekitchn.com/how-to-make-marble-cake-cooking-lessons-from-the-kitchn-191768. Accessed 13 April 2018.

Chapter 12

Bennis, W.G. (2014) quoted in Kandavalli, P. (2014), *Thoughts on Business, Leadership and Christian Life,* Wordpress, https://paulkandavalli.wordpress.com/2014/08/03/warren-bennis-quotes-on-leadership-and-management. Accessed 9 April 2018.

Gray, A. (2017) 'Denmark has the best Work–Life Balance. Here's why', weforum.org, https://www.weforum.org/agenda/2017/03/denmark-best-work-life-balance-oecd/. Accessed 16 April 2018.

Maslow, A. (1971) *The Farther Reaches of Human Nature,* Penguin New York.

OECD (2017) 'Denmark', Better Life report, http://www .oecdbetterlifeindex.org/countries/denmark/. Accessed 16 April 2018).

Riley, P. (2010), *Attachment Theory and the Teacher-Student Relationship,* Routledge.

Seet, C.K. (1961) *Discourses on Buddhism,* Wah Seong Press, Malacca.

VisitDenmark (2018) 'Hygge: The Danish Art of Cosiness', *Tourist Guide,* https://www.visitdenmark.com/denmark-hygge. Accessed 16 April 2018.

Wuthnow, R. (1995) *Learning to Care: Elementary Kindness in an Age of Indifference,* Oxford University Press.

Index